W9-BKP-640

A Rainbow Book

Rainbow Books, Inc.

How To Stay Married Without Going Crazy

Rebecca Fuller Ward, MSW

RAINBOW BOOKS, INC.

Library of Congress Cataloging-In-Publication Data

Ward, Rebecca Fuller, 1942-
   How to stay married without going crazy / Rebecca Fuller Ward.
      p.   cm.
   Includes bibliographical references.
   ISBN 1-56825-048-7 (alk. paper)
   1. Marriage. I. Title.
   HQ734.W26   1999
   306.81--dc21   99-38144
                                                             CIP

How To Stay Married Without Going Crazy

by Rebecca Fuller Ward

ISBN 1-56825-048-7 / softcover / $12.95

Publishing industry inquiries (reviewers, retailers, libraries, wholesalers, distributors/media) should be addressed to:

Rainbow Books, Inc.
P.O. Box 430, Highland City, FL 33846-0430
Editorial Offices—
Telephone: (888) 613-BOOK; Fax: (863) 648-4420; Email: RBIbooks@aol.com

Individuals' Orders: (800) 356-9315; Fax: (800) 242-0036; Online: (http://www.) upperaccess.com, amazon.com, barnesandnoble.com

Printed in the United States of America.

Dedication

For my parents, I. B. and Marian, and my son Dan.

And to Don. For Don. It's always Don.

Contents

It is not marriage that fails; it is people that fail. All that marriage does is to show people up.
—*Harry Emerson Fosdick*

Acknowledgments

Phyllis Anderson has been instrumental in this project. She read every word as I went along, sent encouragement my way, and, at times, gently urged me to "go back and find your voice on this one."

Chapter by chapter she received what was evolving and I cannot thank her enough for her help, advice, unrelenting encouragement and her friendship. She believed I had something to say and told me that often. "Rebecca, you can help people who will never be in your office. Please write this book."

When the struggle to distill got especially frustrating, she would say, "This is not THE book: it's THIS book. Save it for the next one!" She also did the proofing and got the manuscript ready to send out. And Phyllis came up with the title **How To Stay Married Without Going Crazy.** I had started out to write a primer called "Marriage 101." About half-way through the writing process, she e-mailed me the news one day that "we're dumping the Marriage 101. We'll come up with something more applicable to what the book's really about."

She did.

I whined and pled my case, but she was firm. "Give it up; we're not using that title." She held her ground. And she always kept her cool, which is one of her most dependable traits. She also shared my vision.

Phyllis, my dear friend, thank you, thank you.

As you will see in the bibliography, the work of many colleagues I've met or known only through their books are part of the underpinnings for how I work with couples. My own methods have evolved through the years from this amalgamation of books and workshops and articles.

Dr. David Schnarch's work really has been important in my professional life. After my first workshop with him in 1992, I felt like I needed to put a "Closed for Remodeling" sign on my door. His phenomenal work has certainly been an opportunity for my own clinical skills to grow. And growth is both necessary and exhilarating and frustrating, but keeps the work creative and energizing. I also owe thanks to Dr. Lewis W. (Bud) Hyde, my first mentor.

Dear friends emerged to offer their interest and support for a project they didn't get to see. I wondered often if they didn't share concern at times about Rebecca and her "imaginary book." But they were there — Robert, Ruthie, Teri, Nancy, Julia, Janet, Myra, and Susan.

Thanks to my partners Bruce, Jean and Roger for showing enduring interest. Jean's pronouncement, "This is a good book. I need it for my patients," was great encouragement.

Thanks to my family: brother, Bill, and son and daughter-in-law, Dan and Jen. Their presentation of the lovely Caroline Rebecca Smith, our angel baby, in January 1998, stopped the book in its tracks for several months as the role of grandmother took precedence over all others. When they moved to Florida that next June, my broken heart was partially mended by continuing this book.

To the couples who had the courage to walk into my office and confront themselves in my presence I am eternally grateful. Even after 20 years as a therapist, I am always respectful of their willingness to trust both themselves and me as they undertake what is often an arduous journey.

And thanks to Don, my incredible husband. He's not only a scratch golfer; he's a scratch husband. He makes marriage almost easy! He listened to every word, every sentence and every paragraph. And I do mean listened. He endured with his usual adaptability the many nights I was up in the wee hours clicking away. I had a nocturnal muse that played havoc with our normal circadian rhythms for over 18 months. Don — thank you for always being who you are. I've never known anyone more comfortable with himself than you are — and without one hour of psychotherapy. I count on you and adore you. Indeed, you are the wind beneath my wings. You are my hero.

Prologue

The idea for this book began one day about two years ago in the middle of a session with a couple who had been married about 18 months. Both about 30, they were locked into what must have felt like terminal conflict. They were more than discouraged. John interrupted the verbal skirmish, looked at me in anguish and said, "Do we just not know how to be married? Do other couples have this much trouble or is it just us?"

My immediate thought was "No. People don't just know how to be married. They need to learn." And, I thought, I can teach them. Having failed at marriage and having succeeded, I am aware of the difference. And having sat in my office for 20 years with hundreds of couples, I've seen every variety of marital problem. I've observed again and again the baffling and painful knots two people can create for themselves in their marriage. I've observed unresolved conflicts that have smoldered for 30 years and watched less lengthy marriages set themselves up for such misery. What is it about marriage that promotes such intense emotions between two people? The first chapter will deal with this complex, often misunderstood, fascinating, and universal relationship.

This book is not research based. It comes from what I've seen in my office since I began working in 1979. I've seen hundreds of couples during these 20 years and learned from every one of them. Certainly I've learned that being in love or infatuated or attracted to someone may lead you into a marriage but it doesn't teach you "how" to be married. However, those emotional states can absolutely keep you motivated to learn the necessary skills for a healthy marital relationship. And that's what this book is about, the skills you need to acquire so you can eliminate unnecessary problems in your marriage. You can learn how to be married, stay married, stay in love, and not go crazy.

This book will focus on married couples. Marriage is the operative word here. I've seldom found traditional pre-marital counseling of any real value. It's like loaning a pregnant couple someone else's baby for a few days so they can learn what it's like to be a parent. Being able to handle "chores" or duties is part of it, but learning how to navigate and negotiate the emotional issues in marriage (or being a parent) is the first requirement. You don't know how marriage will change you and your partner until you do it. And marriage itself is a catalyst for change. There will be change in both what you expect from "being married" — the state or structure — and change in the expectations you now have of your partner — the relationship. The complexity of the structure and relationship and their interface is what I'll try to clarify in this small volume.

When I was a brand new psychotherapist with lots of book learning and precious little experience, I saw a couple early on Friday mornings. Each week they seemed to have a new problem to deal with and we would devote the hour to finding a solution. It would seem that we did, but the next week there would be a familiarity about the new conflict presented for treatment. I was beginning to catch on to something. Solve one problem and that particular situation may be fixed. Solve the underlying issues driving the conflict and the couple can take care of themselves. It's sleuthing for those hidden emotional agendas lurking just beneath our consciousness that is a challenge and provides the never-ending fascination for me. We all have them, but few of us ever get to the awareness of the "my issue" stage. Often we're too busy looking for an external culprit. Being willing to look at yourself is the first positive prognostic indicator I have.

This book will be useful to people who are able to distance themselves from their spouse and the marriage and take a look at themselves. That ability to view the self in an honest evaluative manner is imperative to being able to utilize the concepts presented here. I often tell couples that a lecture on dental hygiene can be helpful but if you need a root canal you need to go to the dentist. You can get many useful tools in this marriage primer if you are mature enough to take responsibility for yourself and the consequences of your behavior.

Years ago, a newly-wed woman in one of my groups was complaining to group members about the insensitivity of her husband. "He just left me right in the middle of a fight, just walked out and slammed the door," she wailed.

"What had you said to him that made him leave?" one of the members asked.

"Well, I told him to get out," the woman said, only then recognizing her role in the action. She went on to say, "But he should have known that's not what I meant."

Group members immediately nailed her on this and she began to laugh, saying, "I better mean what I say next time." All learned a valuable lesson, including me, who still needs repetition to reinforce my learning.

This will be short not because it couldn't be long but because I didn't want the book to "look" intimidating. I wanted it to appear inviting and accessible so help could be attained quickly. Enjoy and learn.

Rebecca Fuller Ward, MSW

"They dream in courtship, but in wedlock wake."
—*Alexander Pope*

Introduction

Marriage: Why It's So Hard

Water is wet, heat is hot, and marriage is hard. Think about it. Why wouldn't it be? Sharing a life together is an awesome assumption to begin with. I mean, we get tired of people in an elevator and here we are expecting to share all of our most precious resources with another person for 50 or 60 years, preferably in peace and harmony, and absolutely be happy while we're doing it. The notion of having "to work" at marriage is an odious contemplation for most of us who down in our deepest emotional recesses believe that if we loved each other enough, all would flow easily. No real effort would be necessary. There would be no troubles or problems between us, and those difficulties imposed on us by the environment we would meet together in mutual support and attunement. Our disagreements would be rare and trivial and without emotional investment.

Wrong.

The first information I want to share with you is that marriage is difficult. For everyone. Sure, some folks have less difficulty than others do, but it is hard to be married because living with another person is hard. While most people don't come into therapy to deal with a college or apartment roommate, I've heard much about this relationship during my office hours. Living together requires each person to be flexible and adaptable so even roommates have to learn to adapt. They don't have the emotional burdens that spouses carry into the living arrangements.

Living with someone takes some adjusting even if you're not married to him/her. It's not impossible, just difficult. Accepting that as reality and not as anomaly will encourage you to be more open to what this book has to offer.

Why do we get married? And we do marry and often. If one marriage doesn't work, we marry again to someone different, this time hoping the previous selection process was the problem, not us and not the fundamental and inherent difficulty of marriage. When we do marry, we generally make this grandiose commitment propelled by and under the influence of our feelings: transient and fragile emotional states responsive to the weather, hormones, money, music and alcohol, among other stimuli. Most of us can't say what we want for dinner but we promise our spouse we will want him or her forever. And we mean it when we say it. We're under the spell of courtship, a magical interlude in which we view our beloved as perfect and we ourselves have never been so wonderful. People in the throes of courtship are blind, deaf, senseless, and unresponsive to the reality that lies just ahead. One of my longtime patients, a stunningly beautiful woman, is currently single after a second divorce. While single these past five years, she has had a multitude of short-term relationships, relationships that seldom get past the courtship phase. She calls this "the bubble." "Everything is wonderful right now," she reports, "we're in the bubble." And bubbles usually burst, as we all know. There are many people who cannot handle the reality of a relationship outside the protection of the courtship bubble and go from person to person, enjoying the excitement of novelty but not making it very long as courtship fades into relationship. You can imagine how they fare when relationship develops into marriage.

Recognition of our idealized love-object as human after all, sets in about six to eight months later. It's like we "sober" up. Most of us are subject to this unconscious and hormonally-driven hiatus from good judgment and should enjoy it to the fullest. But we probably shouldn't marry until we're safely through it and able to see the beloved without the idealized projections with which we have unconsciously covered them. This projecting process is why later in the throes of marriage we often feel and say, "You're not who I married — you've changed."

The truth is, the beloved who has been on his/her best behavior, probably has relaxed somewhat as you have. Often it's the projections of idealized traits that we've supplied onto the partner that begin to fall off like clothes off a coat hanger with the passage of time and shared experiences that is the bigger culprit in the first disillusionment of marriage. My advice is, "Deal with it." Your partner is real after all just as you are. The growing up begins.

Marriage, if it progresses like it should and we along with it, will grow us right up. It's a catalyst, not an obstacle, to personal maturity, and emotional maturity is a requirement for being happily married. If more of us were maturer when we got married, being married wouldn't be nearly as difficult. Those couples who have less difficulty in adjusting to each other and to the marital situation usually are more self-contained emotionally than those who have more trouble.

I am going to try to not use too many "clinical" terms, but I need to use these two: *enmeshment* and *differentiation*, which mean just what they look like they should mean. If you're enmeshed in something or someone, you've lost your sense of who you are. Your personal boundaries have been violated or permeated, maybe even melted. They no longer are there to help you stay intact. This is not a good thing. You need to know where you start and stop and where your partner starts. I cannot tell you how important having this awareness is in having a healthy intimate relationship. You need always to be aware of your differentness, your separateness from your partner and your partner needs to be aware of his or hers from you. Being able to stay intact even though you're in a close relationship is called differentiation. It's the ability to hang on to yourself while enjoying emotional intimacy and closeness with your partner. And it's imperative that you both are able to stay differentiated. This helps you both not get confused about who feels what, which is crucial to know in your marriage. Many couples have problems with being able to stay individuals when they become emotionally and sexually involved. One or both spouses seem to have a strong need to be able to influence each other's emotional state. Pressure can be strong from an insecure or needy spouse who wants your approval and agreement about his/ her feelings. If you're not clear about who is feeling what or your right to your own emotional response, the boundaries between you and your partner will get stuck together. Then you feel confused, muddled, not sure what is happening and who you are. Communication even feels a little sticky. If I start to feel like I'm talking to Tar Baby or I *am* Tar Baby then I know it's time to check out what I'm doing with my enmeshment/differentiation issues.

The Family of Origin (our FOO that you will read about in Chapter 2) is instrumental in our developing a comfortable level of differentiation. If the emotional boundaries between family members stay clear and each person's feelings are considered and acknowledged, then you will emerge better able to stay separate but close without much anxiety. But if your Family of Origin was enmeshed with each other, you're going to come out of the family with problems keeping good clear boundaries and a firm sense of self. I once had the interesting experience of seeing first one grown daughter, and then her sister, and finally the Mother who had been "in" my office for over a year through the eyes of her daughters. All struggled with being able to be in a relationship and not getting completely lost in the emotional requirements of the partner. Each of the daughters had described the family thus: "When Mother got a headache, we all got headaches, even my brother." This was an enmeshed family. If one family member got a headache, everybody took an aspirin. If one family member was in a bad mood, all family members got into a bad mood. All three siblings had great difficulty in intimate relationships and the oldest, the son, now 44, has never married. Probably a wise decision. His sisters have both had volatile marriages with frequent upheavals and separations.

Being able to hold your ground, to stand firm in your own emotional response is a sign of being differentiated and achieving a necessary level of maturity. I've seen over and over again an emotionally weakened spouse who has spent years being compliant with a demanding partner, who would come in the office depressed, angry, even numb emotionally. He/she will not know "how I feel or even if I feel anything." The years of denying personal feelings has finally produced someone who doesn't even feel. And why would he/she? With the inability to respect and hold onto the self in the presence of an undifferentiated spouse, comes the inevitable diminishing of awareness of feelings. It's just simpler that way. Quit feeling so you don't have to be in conflict with a spouse who wants you to feel just as he/she does.

Except we don't work that way. We are first and foremost emotional beings. We have developed a neocortex along the way and this helps us certainly be able to contain, restrain, and process the emotional responses we are dealing with throughout our lives, but we must respect the power feelings play in our existence. And especially in our relationships. In your relationship, it is necessary for you to honor your own feelings regardless of the pressure your partner may exert to have you feel otherwise. Each of us has to learn to hang on, hold on, and stand firm. Learn to calm and soothe yourself. It's wonderful to have another do that for you, but ultimately you have to be able to do that for yourself. What an achievement when a baby either finds its thumb or learns how to put its pacifier in its mouth! Then it doesn't need mommy or daddy all the time. This "holding on to yourself" is learning to put your own pacifier in if need be.

One of the often heard conflicts I hear from couples arises over the discrepancy in need to "talk to a resolution." One partner is likely to be a "We're going to talk about this NOW and get it over with." And the spouse may need a little time out to process his/her feelings and is not willing to talk NOW. What does the impatient partner seeking an immediate resolution do? Take a deep breath, comfort himself/herself with soothing messages, and wait. Our spouse will not, can not, and should not be expected to always comply with our needs nor we to his/hers. Learning to deal with the frustration when that occurs is something you have to learn. I remember telling my husband one time when he was trying to tease me out of my annoyance at him for being so late from a golf game. He was home, ready to relax and enjoy a Saturday afternoon, and I was ticked. He couldn't talk me out of it and was getting frustrated. "Hey, this may be inconvenient, but I'm mad," I told him. "Just leave me alone for awhile and I'll see what happens, but you're trying to get me over it on your time schedule is not working." He heard me and while he didn't particularly like my mood, he accepted that was where I was and he'd better deal with it. Good for him! Don has struggled with his need for my constant good spirits and has grown enough to stay calm when the vagaries of hormones and life interfere.

So learn to calm and soothe yourself when your partner won't act right! It's a sign of your differentiation, your maturity, and ability to be in a healthy relationship.

Marriage is the ultimate end for relationships in our culture, often culminating a passionate courtship. Someone I can't remember once wrote, "Marriage stops the frenzy of courtship." The moment the people at the end of the aisle utter their intentions, each takes on a new identity: someone's husband or wife, and with those roles comes a daunting array of emotional, physical, financial and social expectations. Some of these expectations the new spouses are aware of and some reveal themselves along the way, generally when one of them has not been met.

One of my repetitions is, "We all have emotional baggage and when we marry, we start unpacking." Here in this legally-sanctioned union, the emotional furies of our past are unleashed.

One fairly young husband stated emphatically to me one day in a joint session, "I'm tired of paying for her crazy mother!" I understood completely.

In marriage, we all have to deal with major issues that are present in most relationships but are much more intense in the marital one. The major issues that present themselves for us to deal with are:

1. *Power and control: Who's in charge here? Is equality possible?*
2. *Emotional Intimacy/Distance: How close can I get? Will I still be me? Where do I stop and my partner start?*
3. *Dependency/Trust: Do I trust my partner to be there for me? Do I trust myself to handle it either way? Will I be there for him/her?*
4. *Affection: How different are we in our needs for affection? How will I ask for what I need? Can I give what my partner needs?*

5. *Self/Marriage: How do I hang on to myself and still be a marital partner?*

There are others but these are core issues that all couples must recognize and deal with.

I was talking one day in session with a couple in mid-marriage (seven to 15 years normally), and the husband said sadly, "I'm tired of compromising. Compromise means neither of us gets what we want."

"Or," I offered, "both of you get some of what you want."

He smiled and replied, "Rebecca, you never give up."

Don't you, either. Marriage is the relationship that offers us the most possibility for growth, connection, and awareness of who we are. It is in the context of relationships that we experience ourselves and marriage is the ultimate context.

Chapter 1

The Golden Rule of Marriage

$\mathcal{L}$essons we really learn are always learned personally. I learned about the Golden Rule of Marriage almost 20 years ago from my personal experiences. I believe I can tell you about it and that you will understand — because you will recognize how you followed it or did not follow it in your own marriage.

Years ago, almost a newly-wed, I got miffed by Don's, (my husband's) lack of consideration for my feelings when he failed to call and let me know he was going to be late coming home. When he finally came in, I promptly let him know how I felt. He was so genuinely surprised by my reaction — he didn't even get defensive.

"I don't understand why you're mad. I wouldn't have been upset if you hadn't called me," he said.

I said, "I am upset whether you understand it or not."

"I treat you like I expect to be treated," he replied, becoming a little defensive and implying I thought that that should be good enough.

"Well, don't," I shot back, "I'm not you."

This discussion led to our establishing the "30 minute" grace period and also the golden rule in our marriage.

The Golden Rule of Marriage is different from the Biblical Golden Rule which advises us to treat (do unto) others as we would like to be treated (done unto). This doesn't work in marriage because your partner isn't you — which you'll continually discover with delightful astonishment (hopefully).

Your partner expects a whole lot more from you than does your car pool, co-workers, golfing buddies, or even your best friend. No one expects as much from any other human being than spouses expect from each other. The Golden Rule of Marriage is to treat your partner the way he/she tells you he/she wants to be treated. And hopefully, he/she will tell you. If not, you're both in trouble.

John and Mary learned the Golden Rule after a miserable few weeks in which Mary had distanced herself with a painful pout and John had withdrawn in confusion not knowing what was going on. Married less than a year, this had occurred after John had been ill. He had had a two-day stomach virus, and he complained, "She wouldn't leave me alone. She was in the bedroom every 10 minutes asking how I felt and what I needed. I needed to be left alone so I could sleep."

"I was trying to help," Mary offered. "When you're sick, you need to be nurtured."

John gave her important information, "To me, being left alone is being nurtured!"

John came from a large family and had shared a room with two brothers. When he got sick as a child, he was put into a bedroom all alone, to heal in solitude and blessed silence.

Mary was from a small family. She was the only daughter and she got treated like a hotel guest when she had even the sniffles. She was propped up in bed and had a mother who checked on her like she was in intensive care. Mary wanted constant attention when she was sick and expected John to need the same.

Each had very different needs around being nurtured when ill and sharing those personal needs was crucial to mutual understanding.

Adopting the Golden Rule of Marriage requires some emotional attributes from each of you. You must be self-aware and know what you need and then be willing to tell your partner who must have the capacity to accept your instructions. Often conflict arises when one of you offers a critical response to what your partner has shared.

"That's ridiculous," or "How in the world could you like/want that?" are two unwise responses. When your partner shares how he/she wants you to treat him/her, listen and don't be critical or judgmental. Sharing what you want is taking a risk and needs to be respected. Reacting with shock, disbelief, and discounting remarks is not helpful in encouraging more risk taking. There is more of this example of poor communication and how to correct it in Chapter 3. But I cannot say this often enough: Never, never discount or invalidate your partner when he/she shares a feeling with you. Not even in the name of reassurance.

I want to tell you about Rob and Maggie. This couple had been married for 25 years when they came in for treatment. The children and helping them solve their problems had protected the relationship from having its own problems for years. The last child had left for college and with no distractions or diversions, each had begun to feel dissatisfied. Both Rob and Maggie valued the marriage and were eager for help. In this session, the focus had been on how well they were able to tell each other what their needs were.

Maggie said to Rob, "I need more affection from you."

This was too general a statement so I asked her to specify how she wanted Rob to be more affectionate.

He asked, "Do you want me to hug and kiss you more? Snuggle? Please tell me how to do this for you."

"I want you to mow the yard," she replied thoughtfully.

Rob looked at me, shaking his head, "How would I have ever figured that out?"

"You wouldn't have," I told him. "Maggie had to tell you."

I love that story because it's a wonderful example of how important it is that you know exactly what you need and be willing to tell your partner in specific, operational terms. Think of all the roses sent when a foot rub was the ticket.

You are responsible for knowing and telling. And remember there is no correlation between depth of love and clairvoyance. No matter how much your partner loves you, he/she cannot possibly know what you want until you tell. You must squeal on yourself. You and your spouse are "wired" differently.

A good bit of the time, we don't understand our own wiring, so we must not expect our partner to grasp this very complex emotional condition. This myth of "if you loved me, you'd know" persists, and I want you to give it up. Let it go. Hanging onto it diminishes your effectiveness and denies responsibility for taking care of yourself, which you have to do when you're mature. And you know it takes mature people to be married.

My husband and I will soon celebrate our 19th wedding anniversary and we both enjoy our relationship immensely. Recently, after I had shared something personal with him about "wants and needs," he began explaining to me that since he didn't want or need this, I shouldn't either.

"What is the Golden Rule of Marriage?" I asked him.

First he looked puzzled, then he smiled and said, "Treat your partner like she wants to be treated all the time."

"Not all the time," I told him, "just enough of the time."

Chapter 2

The FOO Issue

*"When a man and a woman are married their romance
ceases and their history commences."*
—Rochebrune

FOO stands for "family of origin," and therapists really like to "go there" in our work because it is in
the family that so much of who we are was cast. The FOO
is where we came from, and to understand your family is
to know yourself. Information I need early on and ask for
of each spouse is "Tell me about your parents' marriage.
Did they have the kind of marriage you wanted?"

Our parents' marriage, like it or not, is the prototype
for our own relationship. And interestingly enough, we tend
to replicate it in some fashion. Discovering how we've done
this is very useful.

I think we've all experienced many times a feeling of
disbelief when our spouse has responded, reacted, re-
quested, and/or refused some behavior we thought perfectly reasonable. I've seen hundreds of time in the office
that look of sheer amazement when the partner reveals
his/her shocking deviant approach to life.

"What do you mean? I don't understand why getting
an artificial Christmas tree is such a big deal," or "Why
can't we eat dinner Thanksgiving dinner at two instead of
noon?" or "Well, at my house my dad always had a drink

before dinner and never took his dishes to the kitchen."

And I've had spouses tell me about their partner's family as if they were describing some tribe of primitives whose bizarre rituals should be studied. It's like "culture shock" as we realize that our partner who is also a Methodist or who's mother was my mother's college roommate or who also grew up in our hometown also grew up in a family very different from our own.

"Well, in HER family" or his, the spouse begins, and I know I'm about to hear something the informer considers, well, at least, peculiar.

This is all legitimate stuff. Knowing about our own "beginning" is in my opinion crucial to living an aware existence; learning about our partner's beginning is necessary for a good marriage. It is in our childhood that our ability to love and trust was nurtured or not, and that affects our marital relationship directly. It is in our family of origin — our FOO — that we learned what emotions were okay to have and to talk about and which ones were better left unmentioned and in some cases left unfelt. All this emotional wiring is done without our permission. We are unwitting participants.

My first paper in graduate school was on "The Nature of Man" and my opening sentence was "Man is a victim." My professor thought I was cynical but I think I was accurate. We are all victims of circumstance in that we have no choice in selecting our parents or the conditions emotionally, physically or psychologically that will surround our development.

But unwitting or not, for the rest of our lives we have to deal with what happened to us from birth to adulthood and mostly how it affects our ability to be in relationships. I tell all my patients that we are all recovering children and learning what we are recovering from is essential to personal growth and responsibility.

Here is a case example of how the early training is

precursor to the dynamics in our marital relationship.

Cal and Marian, early 50's, are in my office with huge problems around "communication." This is their second marriage, and each has grown children and baby grandchildren. His first wife died and her husband died suddenly some years after their divorce. Each is successful, attractive and opinionated. Not only are they dealing with the early wiring issues but also the first marriage influences. They actually communicate, i.e., have fluent verbal skills, very well.

Their problem is they don't like what they are hearing! Cal is a very high profile litigator, used to being listened to and obeyed. Marian is a well-trained nurse, now in an administrative position where folks listen and follow her instructions.

These two titans are clashing regularly as each struggles for control. In getting FOO information, I discover interesting, as always, dynamics.

He is the adored first born and only son and she is the first born, oldest of three girls, and the identified "show child." Her mother, one of the first female doctors in her home state, was a strong dominant woman who was CEO of the family and Marian's definitive role model. She described her family as "warm, loving, and always talking about everything.

"I never felt like my feelings, any of them, were suspect," Marian said.

Cal's father was the head of the house he grew up in and his mother "stayed home and took care of us and the house. She adored my father and they never argued." They never talked much about their emotions, according to Cal, and the focus was on "doing, not being" in his home.

Well, you can see how these early templates are affecting this couple in the present. Both are simply playing out what they know to be normal and expected. As they talked to each other about what they learned about male-female relationships based on their prototypes, they could see how early influences were guiding responses in the present and were able to re-do some of the early decisions.

Here are some FOO questions for you to ponder as you begin to see yourself as your spouse's marital partner:

1. *Who made the decisions in your family of origin?*
2. *How did your parents resolve conflict?*
3. *Who did you talk to when you had a problem? When you were sad or hurting in some way, whom did you turn to?*
4. *How did Mom and Dad handle anger? Sadness?*
5. *Who did you depend on? Who was reliable?*
6. *Were you allowed to be angry? Sad? How did you express your feelings?*
7. *Did your feelings matter to your parents? Did they listen to your opinions?*
8. *Did you feel valued in your family?*
9. *How was love and appreciation expressed in your FOO?*
10. *What traits did you like and dislike most about each parent?*
11. *Was your growing-up house a happy house to be in?*
12. *How did you get your way?*

There are many others but these should help you discover a little about the culture you were exposed to as a child. The environment and circumstances of your family were instrumental in your development. And your partner had the same process occurring but in another family. He/she grew in a different "garden" and both of you need to know this and accept this so you don't feel that your partner is just trying to drive you crazy. It is not information you can take or leave. Learning about yourself and your partner is necessary to attain the level of awareness and understanding necessary to reach the collaborative stage of marriage (see Chapter 8).

These next few paragraphs are very important. I want to introduce you to the concept of "Different but not wrong," or "Different but not right."

Couples really seem to have difficulty with their differences. I believe the healthier you emerged from your FOO training the better able you are to tolerate when your partner is different from you and you don't feel the need to get into the "right or wrong" contest. Remember you came from different FOO's and what you learned there is on the hard-drive.

I used to say to my puzzled partner somewhat flippantly, "Welcome to MY world!" when he was stunned by a behavior and/or viewpoint that seemed normal and customary to me.

He would respond similarly with his, "Yeah, well in Wardsville, we always ate the feathers." Over the years he has recognized that our differences are not meant to be insulting or challenging. It's simply that we are different. Period.

When you and your spouse are experiencing technical difficulties because of a "being different" situation, slow down, take a deep breath. Remind yourself that it's okay for you two to be un-alike. Your relationship is not being threatened.

Listen to the differences. You will not be annihilated. No character slurs or name-calling is necessary. Let your maturity show as you and your partner display your separateness.

Some excellent advice is not to criticize your partner for how, where and with whom he/she grew up. Their FOO and your FOO are not your fault. You may think your spouse's family would be a life's work for an ambitious anthropologist, but don't share this information with your spouse. Keep it a secret. Or tell a trusted friend. Generally, most of us will defend our FOO vigorously against criticism and/or judgment from our partner even if we agree with it! It's just the way it is. Be very careful when you venture into that area. Respect the deep emotional attachments each of you have to your family and honor the experience each of you received in that family.

Again I tell all my patients that we are all recovering children and learning what we are recovering from is essential to personal growth and responsibility.

In closing this chapter on the all important FOO issue, let me add a bit about new marriages. Often newlyweds have the most difficulty with FOO influences and differences. Those are primary bonds and were there long before the spouse, so initially they can exert more power. The marriage is new; the FOO is old. This past week I had a young couple in who are struggling to establish their own FOO and have a new baby to promote this development. Married for only three years, their FOO's are very, very different. Jack's family practiced "emotional non-events" as a way of life. Communication about feelings was discouraged in both subtle and overt ways while Angie's family loved to "wallow in our emotions," she says.

"We talked about everything and anything most of the time." Now married to a man who has little awareness of his own feelings much less how to share them, she finds herself still turning to her FOO for support.

Jack is threatened by her need to be in contact with them so often and complained that "She talks to her mother at least five times a day. She even asks her what kind of toilet paper to buy!"

I suggested to him that as his wife learns through experience that he will be available when she needs emotional connection, she will turn to him more and more.

"Be patient and be available," I advised.

Each is living according to the customs in their FOO and will soon discover that as they share information about their prior lives, they will grow to understand each other and be less threatened when the differences appear. The struggle to discover how their family is going to be will be less painful as they blend experiences and preferences by open communication. Again, being different will only cause you trouble if you let it.

"Marriage is difficult. For everyone."
—R. Ward

Chapter 3

Communication: The Universal Complaint

*M*arriage is responsible for many profound changes and I believe this because so many people tell me it is.

According to many of the couples who have come in for treatment, the state of marriage has altered significantly the personalities of their mates. I hear frequently how formerly desirable, sensitive, interesting, communicating partners have under the influence of the marital state become practically deaf and mute strangers driving the still intact partner into therapy.

About 97 percent of the couples who come for therapy (with the deaf, mute strangers they have married), come because of a "communication problem." This is their diagnosis and after listening to them for a few minutes I generally agree. But from the outset I introduce the notion that what they are experiencing is more of an emotional problem.

Emotional Aphasia is the inability to articulate feelings and can affect couples tremendously. The condition can strike without warning and last for hours, days, weeks and even years. The affected couple will become more and more distant and the relationship will suffer. In the case of the emotional aphasia lasting for months or years, a relationship can be irrevocably damaged. I'm not talking about a "pout" situation. I'm addressing the persistence of one or both spouses being unable or unwilling to share feelings with the other until a feeling of hopelessness about the relationship "ever working" develops.

While your ability to share verbally has diminished under the influence of marriage, your ability to decipher non-verbal language has increased exponentially. Couples become experts at decoding facial expressions, gestures, and body posture of the partner. You know when your spouse is mad long before I do.

Sid and Toni are a good example of how powerful non-verbal language can be. They are both in their late 30's and have been married about four years, a first marriage for each. The session is barely beginning when Toni blurts out, "There! Did you see it? That look, I hate it. He's mad and wants me to shut up."

I'm clueless and so is Sid. He says, "I don't have any idea what she's talking about. She accuses me all the time. What look? I'm not doing anything. She's crazy."

While I have not observed "the look," Toni has. Sid may or may not know he's got "the look," but something just happened and they both need to figure it out.

Also, "tone" is a word I hear much about with couples struggling to communicate. "It's not what you said, it's how you said it," or "I could tell by your tone that you were upset," are frequently said in my office.

Years ago this wonderfully authoritarian physician was brought to my office by his frustrated wife. He was not thrilled to be there but was willing because he was intelligent enough to know that he and his wife were having grave communication problems. Her complaint was his "tone of voice."

"He talks to me like I am a scrub tech in the OR, not

his wife," she said. She had told him over and over that it wasn't "what" he said, but "how" he said it, his tone of voice.

He had replied in all seriousness, "I don't do tones!" His wife had begged to differ and found help for them both. To his credit, he learned all about non-verbal communication including "tones" and he and his wife have not been back since their initial treatment. He has remained sensitive to his tone of voice since.

Of course, we talk in a certain "tone" of voice and mastering congruency, tone that reflects meaning, is crucial to clear communication with your spouse. If your partner is affected by your "tone of voice," rather than spring to defend yourself by offending your partner, get curious and ask, "What did I sound like? I need you to help me hear what I'm doing that is blocking communication." (This is "collaboration." More on that is in Chapter 8.)

While we might not be aware of our "tone," we all need to strive to be aware of it, as it is a crucial factor in communicating clearly. Think of the way Jerry Seinfeld communicates his loathing of his neighbor by simply saying his name, one word, "Newman," which he says with tight lips and sarcasm dripping off every letter. Tone is a powerful tool. You can learn about how you use it from your partner who can be an excellent teacher.

I am continually impressed with how determined and creative couples can be about not expressing themselves to each other consistently (sucking in expression until there is a blow-up is not a healthy pattern). Partners generally do better with sharing information than sharing emotions, they report more easily than they self-disclose, and the emotions they have the most difficulty sharing are anger and need. About this reporting versus revealing, let me confuse you with an example which shows how complicated it can really be.

Ron and Karen came into the office in major distress

because he wouldn't tell Karen when he would be home in the evening. (He wouldn't "share/exchange information.") Married just about a year, they felt locked into a painful stalemate. Ron's position was, "I'm not reporting in to anyone. I'm not a kid and I can come home whenever the hell I feel like it." He felt Karen was trying to control him with her demand that he let her know "when."

It wasn't a control issue for Karen who had a "need to know." "I don't want to tell you when to come home, I just want to know when you're coming," she said.

Karen had been raised by two alcoholic parents and had painful memories of standing in front of elementary school waiting to be picked up by parents who sometimes made it on time and sometimes didn't make it at all. A teacher would call her grandparents to come for her or would take Karen home herself. Karen's issue was not about control and when Ron heard her tearfully recall these painful experiences, his position shifted and he was able to change his behavior to accommodate his wife's need.

Ron had a rigid, authoritarian father in his background who kept tight control over the family so Ron's "rebellion" about having to report in or to be home at a certain time is also understandable.

While Ron and Karen's communication problem seemed to be about exchanging information, there were emotional influences that had to be considered.

All marital communication is affected by the on-going resolved and unresolved emotional issues flowing like a river over, under and between the spouses. The more resolved issues, the less treacherous communicating with each other is. I want to present here the most common mistakes I see couples make while trying to talk to each other. There are many I could present, but these are the ones I see over and over again.

1. *Failing to acknowledge partner's feelings*

2. *Being indirect*
3. *Attributing, Assuming, Analyzing*
4. *Making "You" Statements*
5. *Using Absolutes (red flag words)*

Now I'll describe them and more importantly present solutions.

Acknowledging Feelings: This step in communicating HAS TO HAPPEN. If it doesn't, communication is derailed and recovery is difficult. This acknowledging skill has to do with being able to LISTEN. Lou says to Jay: "I'm feeling very unimportant to you. When you get home late four nights in a row, I don't get any time with you."

Jay replies: "That's ridiculous. I can't help working late."

Lou is unacknowledged, probably feels discounted, and her next response will likely reflect her hurt and anger.

Jay didn't acknowledge her feelings. This has to happen immediately before true dialogue will proceed. We all want above all to be heard and understood by others and especially our spouses. Mature adults can tolerate mere acceptance, which is sometimes all your partner can offer.

Jay's acknowledging response would be "I'm so sorry you feel unimportant to me. Please talk to me about this," or "I don't want you to feel unimportant. You are always important to me and I want you to feel that."

It must be difficult for couples to do this acknowledgment piece because I have to go over it again and again with most. If you can learn to LISTEN to what the partner says, hang on to yourself while the partner talks, do not become defensive or explanatory and respond with a simple, "I hear what you're saying," that's how you do it. It doesn't matter that you think what your spouse has shared is ridiculous, unbelievable, illogical, inhuman, ignorant, and so forth. You do not judge feelings. You acknowledge them. Trust me. You have to learn to do this piece.

Being Indirect: This way of poor communication is so universal between marital partners that I no longer think it's pathological. Indirectness is related to emotion and need.

We are more likely to be indirect when we really need or want something than when we don't. If I am really in dire need of a hug, I am much more likely to be anxious about asking for one than if I'm not very needy. The risk factor rises in direct proportion to our level of need.

Also we are less likely to communicate directly if we are feeling angry or hurt. Anger is scary and being hurt makes us feel too vulnerable. The most common way of being indirect is the use of questions and "Why?" questions are the worst offenders because they tend to promote defensiveness: "Why are you wearing that tie?" or "Why didn't you call me today?"

Don't hide behind a question. Make an "I" statement instead. "I don't like that green tie with the plaid shirt." "I wish you had called me today. I like talking to you during the day." Questions can be a tactic — even unconsciously — to deflect responsibility onto the partner who usually recognizes the maneuver (even unconsciously) and responds accordingly. Using "I" statements shows your colors before your partner has to show his/hers.

For example, say, "I'm hungry for Italian tonight. What sounds good to you?" This will stop the following universal yet miserable exchange.

Mary: "Where do you want to eat tonight?"

John: "I don't care. You pick one." Mary suggests three restaurants and John nixes them all.

Mary becomes frustrated. "Just tell me what you want and we'll go there."

John again: "I don't care, really, you pick."

She does and John is negative again. "For someone who doesn't care, you sure seem to. Forget it, I'm eating a bowl of cereal."

Questions such as, "Do you have a busy day today?" when you really want to ask your partner to do an errand for you is another "indirect indiscretion." Speak up. Ask directly. Hints and waiting for your spouse to read your mind is unproductive.

Snooping is also an odious method of not confronting. It often backfires, i.e., you find the car payment in the glove compartment of your husband's truck. Now what? Do you confront directly or set him up, i.e., "Honey, did you get the car payment mailed?"

My best advice comes from my English teaching days: Noun-Verb-Object.

"I want chocolate now." I added the adverb.

Now get more risky. " I want you to cook now."

"I want you to be neater."

"I need a favor."

"I like jewelry."

"I am playing golf tomorrow." You get the drift. Use direct simple sentences that communicate about you.

Assuming and Analyzing: Do not assume you know what your partner is up to emotionally, cognitively or behaviorally. Ask him/her. Your partner needs the opportunity to respond to whatever you've conjured up.

For example, Mary: "I think you're helping me with the dishes because you plan to deer hunt this weekend and are trying to get in my good graces."

John: "Well, you're close. I bought a new gun and wanted to better my position before telling you. Actually I'd like to go in two weeks while you're away."

Or . . .

Mary: "You've been so quiet tonight. Are you mad about the car?"

John: "What car?" It is dangerous to act on assumptions as if they were reality, but couples do it rampantly.

As one beleaguered spouse shared, "I don't even feel like I'm present at times. He's having a conversation with me and I haven't said a word. He just keeps telling me what I'm feeling and doing. I told him that I was leaving the premises because he sure didn't need me there to talk with; he could do it all by himself." I see that in the office routinely.

Analysis is when one partner plays therapist to the other, i.e., "You're really getting paranoid," or "That behavior is compulsive," or worse, "You are a very sick person." Often after the diagnosis, there is the "treatment plan," such as, "You need professional help." None of this is received graciously.

Analyzing your partner is a carved-in-stone NO-NO. Even I don't get that privilege in my own home. A few times early in my marriage, when I would offer him the benefit of my professional expertise, my husband would look at me rather menacingly and announce, "I didn't hire you, won't pay you, and am not interested in your analysis."

To wit: Marty, half of a 30-year marriage, was prone to frequently analyze his wife Jackie who never received or appreciated his trouble. "Well," he'd say, "you're just like your mother who never could be on time either. Your problem with procrastination is because you fear failure," or "Jackie, I worry your apathy is because you're a depressive."

The man was relentless, though Jackie never responded well to his unsolicited analysis. I wouldn't have either. It was less threatening for Marty to talk about her than reveal himself and his issues.

My husband told me not to include **"attribution"** because he said he didn't understand what it was. It's a little like assumptions but is usually verbalized in the unwise "You" statement. It means "to assign or ascribe as a quality or trait."

Couples do it all the time. They assign often-negative

traits to the partner and then behave as if the assignment were real. And some of the time in can be, at least partially. Traits often assigned are selfishness, inconsiderateness, craziness, rudeness, alcoholism, bitchiness, assholiness, and traits that belong to a family member, usually one with a bad reputation. "You're just like your Uncle Ben," who would be the one in prison for embezzlement. Don't do it. Trust me, it won't help.

Using "You" statements: During courtship, of course, most of our observations about each other are positive. However, once we marry, the observations can be pretty nasty. It's as if the first word bursting out of our mouths in an angry exchange is most often "You" and it's generally followed by one of the above (assumption, analysis, or attribution) resulting in a character assassination or inflammatory insult.

I can make a solution very simple: Only make "You" statements when a compliment follows. The intent is to make your partner feel good. Speak expertly about yourself only. *Use the basic building block of clear communication, the "I" statement. I feel, I need, I want, I think, I am aware.*

Instead of saying, "You're selfish," (inflammatory), say, "I don't feel considered." Instead of, "You're a jerk," (really inflammatory), say, "I'm tired of not getting my way." Do not try, "I feel you're a jerk" either. This is a "You" statement in disguise and will never get by your alert partner. It shouldn't. "I" statements are about you, so stick to the subject.

Using absolutes: The red flag words — words that will trigger a defensive response in your partner — are words like "Always, Never, Should, Should've." These are guaranteed to cause trouble in your communication.

These words will stop the flow on the spot as your partner takes issue. "I am not always late," or "I do too pick up my towel sometimes." Avoid them to avoid a pesky detour in your conversation.

Also be very careful with other all-inclusive words such as everybody, as in, "Well, everybody says you're selfish," or "No one but you liked that movie." While you may be trying to make a point, you might want to assess whether it's worth it or not. "BE RIGHT!" is an affliction many have and my best experience is, "You can be right but you'll probably be alone."

Remember, you always have an emotional agenda when you begin talking. We all do. The problem is, we rarely know clearly what it is because we don't take the time to figure it out. Knowing helps you communicate exactly what you mean to say. (Say what you mean, mean what you say.)

There are many opportunities for mistakes between your transmitter and your partner's receiver. Not knowing yourself what you're really wanting when you begin to speak increases those glitch-ops.

For example, Leslie was worried about money, a usual condition for this 43-year-old teacher married for 15 years to Gary, who worked with his father in a small family business. Gary was prone to avoid any possible conflict so often left unsaid information that would have helped Leslie understand their financial situation better. Often she would begin asking him question after question seeking information, she thought, but she was really needing reassurance from him. And, of course, she didn't often receive it because he was angry at the inquisition approach she was using. Her awareness of what she really needed helped her ask for it directly and Gary responded because he didn't feel attacked.

Taking responsibility for how and what you communicate to your partner will encourage your feelings of differentiation, individuality, and improve the relationship in all areas. Couples have a lot to talk about and it's amazing to me how many ways they find to either not do it or do it poorly. Using just the tools here in this chapter will make a difference.

Marriage —
"The bloom or blight of all men's happiness."
—Byron

Chapter 4

Sex

There is sex after marriage no matter what you've heard. However, sex in a marriage is a compli- cated issue. Couples who come in the office saying, "We have a sexual problem," usually have a relationship prob- lem. Unless there is a physiological basis for equipment failure or malfunction, the couple who is having difficulty relating to each other sexually is having difficulty relating to each other, period.

Sex in marriage is related to everything else going on in the marriage — from daily expressions of appreciation and affection to whether the yard got mowed or the dry cleaning got fetched. Sexual expression is now encumbered by the complexities of emotional needs and expectations and the response by the partner to those needs and ex- pectations. Marriage itself is an encumbering situation and while sex is a crucial element ("the opiate of the married") it will be the first activity to go when the relationship hits a snag, because women will not participate. Some men will not participate either if the relationship is snagged, but more men will than won't. This is not a value judg- ment here. I think it is an interesting evolutionary and physiological observation.

My observations in the office lead me to conclude that most couples have great difficulty communicating about sex. While a partner will give you detailed instructions about how and where to scratch his/her back ("Up, to the right, no, down, a little more, ahhh. That's it."), he/she will absolutely withhold vital information about where and how to touch him/her sexually. Sex lives are severely hampered when partners aren't willing to share their sexual needs with each other, i.e., how they want to be touched, where they want to be touched, and when.

Couples appear to have lots of problems with when they have sex and I think it's because of the initiation factor. Who will take the risk? Sexual rejection is particularly painful and some folks cannot tolerate it, so often the pair will settle into a safe routine with one partner being the designated hitter. Or there will be an unspoken schedule they follow such as sex on specific days, i.e., "We always have sex on Sunday afternoon," or "We never have sex during the week." Or even, "We have sex every other night." Once again I bring up the maturity factor. Take responsibility for initiating lovemaking and trust yourself enough to know you can handle rejection if that's what happens. Waiting for something or someone to make it happen leads to resentment.

Of course, the FOO influence is always instrumental in our acceptance of our own sexuality and our capacity to enjoy its expression. My advice about how to improve your sex life is to take a look at how you feel about your own sexuality. What messages did you get in your FOO about sex? Who gave you information about sex? Usually parents give us information about "reproductive sex" rather than the sex that is driven by both hormonal and emotional desire. When you asked questions about sex, how did your parents respond?

I've teased my mother for years about my own sex education which even by 1950ish standards was sparse. She put a book called **The Stork Didn't Bring You** right in the middle of my bed about two days after I had gotten some garbled information about menstruation from an older playmate and had come to her for information. A few days after the book appeared, I came down to breakfast and she asked, "Did you find the book? You don't have any questions do you?"

"No, I don't," I responded compliantly. As you might think, sex in my family was a taboo subject and I grew up curious about it but definitely fearful of it. Your parents' attitude about sex was instrumental in the formation of your own.

Men and women are different in their sexual needs and expression of those needs as if you hadn't already figured this out. Emotional influences are far more important to most women than hormonal influences, and I think men have more hormonal stimuli than emotional. Through the years I've observed without judgment a husband's ability to let sex drive overcome anger or other negative emotions.

"Yeah, I'm mad she didn't get the car tags like she promised, but, hey, I'm in the mood for love."

Very few wives I've worked with are willing to engage sexually if the partner has misbehaved in some way. Women are wired with direct circuitry from the emotional system to the sexual desire system. With men, the connection doesn't appear to be as direct. This is an observation, not a criticism. Check it out with your own partner to see if it's valid.

In a marriage, sex is not just a biological occurrence. It is intricately related to the emotional balance in the relationship as well as to the business and practical application of running a marriage. I don't often have couples complaining about inorgasmia if they're facing a financial crisis or illness. The old adage "women have to feel close to be sexual and men have to have sex to feel close" is generally true in my experience.

If you notice you're not having sex enough (and your "enough" is entirely your call), scan the emotional part of your relationship. Do you feel close or distant emotionally? Are you current with what your partner has going on in his/her life? Are you looking at each other when you talk? Are you mad about something you've not resolved? What's your "Grudge Index" doing? Many couples who come in for counseling got there because of their "hold then blow" pattern of dealing with conflict (see Chapter 7) which gives them an ongoing level of resentment/anger. Are you each expressing affection with each other? If either of you are "scorekeepers," what's the score? Again, some couples' awareness of "the score" being even (fair) or uneven (unfair) will keep them from having sex.

As you get in touch with what's going on emotionally in your marriage, ask your partner to do it with you. This invitation is a move toward intimacy both emotionally and sexually.

Let me tell you about Penny and Jeff, a couple I saw some years ago. They were in their middle 30's, had four children close in age including a toddler, and each had a demanding occupation. With little time for each other, the relationship had become distant and conflicted. They were distant and conflicted in their sexual relationship as well. She wouldn't have sex with him until she began to feel more emotionally connected and needed both the time for her to share her feelings with him and he to be more emotionally forthcoming than he had been. He wasn't going to take that risk until he felt close and he needed sex to feel close to her. He wanted to eat, she wanted to cook, and neither had a recipe.

Over a three-year period with almost weekly sessions, (Does that kind of commitment give you pause?), they started to understand one another as long unexpressed feelings were expressed. They made time for each other. One day Penny came in alone and said, "I've decided to ***** his socks off! Even though he still isn't talking as much as I want, I see he cares enough to come here every week and work on us. I can bend a little knowing I am important to him."

Well, she did and then he did and they were on their way. I often kidded Jeff, who referred to me as "that woman" during their first year of treatment, that I did have a name and it wasn't Pandora. Only into the second year did I gain some credibility and a name. They are still married as I write.

Many of us marry with very unrealistic expectations of what and how marital sex should be. The operative word here is unrealistic. The most common unrealistic expectations I have observed in the office are these:

1. *I can have (am entitled to) sex whenever I want to now that I'm married.*
2. *My partner is responsible for meeting all my sexual needs.*
3. *If I or my partner don't have an orgasm, one or both of us have performed poorly and the encounter was a dismal failure.*
4. *Sex is not related to anything other than physical need or want.*
5. *Having simultaneous organisms indicates perfect sexual compatibility.*

I'm not serious about this last one although I did see the couple whose definition of good sex was simultaneous orgasms. "Our sexual encounter on Saturday was successful," the husband would proudly report. Of course, it all sounded a bit tedious to me as they described their diligent attention to the progress each was making toward orgasm. Made me think of audibles given at the line of scrimmage. Simultaneous orgasms occur both spontane- ously and with careful planning and communication. They are great fun but certainly no indication of your sexual compatibility or expertise. Please don't put requirements such as this on your sexual relationship. Making love is not about synchronized ecstasy.

You've read the preceding paragraphs, so you now know that sex is related to everything going on in your and your partner's life including outside influences and pressures. Maturity is accepting this as reality. You know that you will have sex with your partner when your partner is avail- able. Hopefully, you see how important it is to know what he/she needs to be available.

Your partner is responsible for meeting many of your sexual needs but he/she will not be able to meet them all. Maturity is accepting this. Some fantasies will not be met though I encourage you and your partner to move some beyond discomfort and embarrassment to see what you can experience with each other sexually.

Take a deep breath and prepare yourself, married people do masturbate. And it's okay. You can, too. I've seen many couples through the years who have had sex daily because one partner desired this. The wife in one of these pairs complained that she was tired of "submitting" every- day and asked for advice. I started talking about mastur- bation as a viable option and she quickly told me "I would feel betrayed if he did that."

"Well, it's you or him," I replied. She chose herself to betray, and I'm not certain this marriage will ever be a healthy one — or even last.

As for the importance of orgasms, let me say that sex is about so much more than muscle contractions. I'm not discounting that wonderful physical experience and I wish many orgasms for you all, but I think if the focus is on this event, you can miss so much of what else is going on. Rather than attend to the performance of your equipment I would encourage the focus to be on how you're using your equipment to be close. Sex is such a regressive private experience between two people and has such possibilities for increased personal and relational growth, I don't want you to limit yourselves to performance criteria.

I'm going to close this chapter with another story of a couple I'm currently seeing that I think will include much of what I've tried to say.

When Carolyn and Mike came in, their complaint was familiar: we don't communicate, we don't have anything in common, we never spend any time together, and we never have sex. (The sex complaint was Mike's). Married for 11 years, they are both 33 with two elementary school age children. One has been diagnosed with ADHD (Attention Deficit Hyperactive Disorder) and is a difficult child who takes lots of time. Carolyn and Mike both work and have since they married. She has steadily progressed in her work environment while Mike has had several jobs and some periods of unemployment. While they both have earned about the same amount of money, Carolyn has always been the consistent breadwinner and managed their finances. This is important though neither one presented it as a factor initially.

They had been separated about two weeks when they came in for their first appointment. Mike's announcement that he was unhappy and wanted to be out of the house had stunned Carolyn and though she complied with his wishes, she felt hurt and betrayed. In the sessions, Mike complained often that he was tired of not having sex and that he didn't "feel loved."

Her complaints were more around emotional intimacy and time issues.

As we explored their relationship, I could see their pattern of come together/pull apart. Going back into the FOO influences, it was easy to see how each had somehow recreated instrumental parts of the parental marriage. This exploration helped each see that their partner was much more complicated that he/she had thought and that their relationship had problems more intricate than they had imagined.

Carolyn's lack of sexual desire for Mike was tied into both security and self-esteem issues. While she had never verbalized her feelings clearly, she felt he had failed to take financial responsibility so she didn't trust him to care for her or the children. She had great difficulty saying to him that this "failure" affected her feelings of respect for him and she didn't feel sexual toward a man she didn't respect. His periods of unemployment had frightened her. He was not "acting like a husband and father are sup-posed to act," comparing him to her father who had been the only breadwinner in her FOO and who had been chief financial officer. Carolyn also resented Mike's choosing to spend so much time with the kids and not making time for her. His lack of attentiveness toward her affected her self-esteem and she began to spend more time with co-work-ers who did seem to find her interesting and fun to be with.

Mike who had been heavy into the "victim" role during most of the sessions, began to listen to her and take some responsibility for the status of his marriage and his sex life. He began to see that sex was not just a biological drive. Carolyn needed more than being told what she was sup-posed to do for him sexually, the old "my right, your duty" attitude. He seemed to have retained from his parents' marriage a conflict-avoidance stance that also makes him intimacy avoidant. When talking about his parents, he described them as "traditional" and said he had never heard them argue. Somewhere in some obscure brain cells of his was the belief that married couples don't argue. During the sessions, I have encouraged confrontation and he is coming along. While he is taking responsibility for his behavior, he is also behaving more responsibly and more actively. As he became more active, Carolyn was able to "under function" which was a relief to her.

At this point in their treatment, they are still separated but are seeing more of each other as a couple. The healing is happening as each takes personal responsibility for his/her contribution to the shape of the marriage.

I want to address how important flexibility and openness are in your sexual relationship. Just as you're going to be hungry for different foods or drinks or kinds of entertainment and intellectual stimulation, you're going to have different sexual desires. There are so many ways to relate to each other sexually. For example, I saw a couple in their middle 40's who were having and had been having a struggle with sex for many years. It was around his insistence that every sexual encounter include the same activities, from foreplay to climax. He wanted first this behavior and then that behavior and a little of this, some more of that, and now time for another tried and true routine. The whole experience lasted well over an hour and he wouldn't consider any variation. Consequently, his wife often feigned a headache or worse to avoid the time and energy commitment he demanded. Often she would offer a "quickie" or a "maintenance session" but he was rigid about what he wanted.

"I don't want sex with you. I want us to make love," he would tell her. After several months in treatment, he began to explore his need to control how their sex life was conducted and why he was so resistant to any of his wife's suggestions. Relinquishing control wasn't easy for him and experimenting with new ways to relate sexually with his wife was anxiety producing, but he was willing to work on this problem and together they found how much fun it could be to enjoy sex in a variety of ways. Recognize that sexual needs will vary and being able to share with your partner what you want or need from him/her sexually in the present will increase your intimacy before you start.

It is always exciting for me as a therapist to see this growth. When people can truly take responsibility for their behavior rather than affix blame, they are becoming mature, the magic ingredient in successful relationships.

Take responsibility for your sex life. It is a vital part of your relationship. Talk about it. Then talk some more. It's okay to be anxious or embarrassed. Trust yourself to tolerate these rather unpleasant feelings. In my own experience, embarrassment has always meant growth for me. I don't let it stop me and I don't want you to let it keep you from growing.

"Marriage has many pains but celibacy has no pleasures."
—*Samuel Johnson*

Chapter 5

Time and Money

I want to reassure you that you're normal if you and your spouse are having problems dealing with time and money issues. And I want to give you some perspective on why you might be having difficulty and some concepts that might help you minimize the problems.

You can count on having conflict over time and money. Do not worry that you've mismarried because you do. Time and money are both about seemingly finite entities (although you can generally make more money) and couples will have strong ideas and opinions about how each wants to allocate them. It's very personal. Think about it. Life's most precious resource is time and society's seems to be money and now you've got to share both with another person who is apt to not always agree with you on how to spend them.

People generally have very strong preferences about how they're going to spend their time and their money and getting married doesn't change those feelings. However, expressing them clearly seems to be difficult. I've seen too many couples struggle with these issues to think it's anything but the norm to struggle.

Time issues revolve around quantity: "How much time are you going to spend with me? With your friends? With just yourself? How are you going to divvy up the hours so I get my fair share? And what is my fair share?"

"Time is the currency of love," I read somewhere years ago and the couples I've worked with certainly validate that statement.

"If you love me, you'll spend time with me. Words are cheap. What are we doing together today?"

After identifying "quantity" as one important element in settling time issues, "quality" is the next to consider. "What are we going to do when we're together? How are we going to make this time together really count?" While you can certainly have quality without quantity, you have to have enough time to let this happen. If you're feeling time deprived, you're likely to focus and fuss about that and I'm not sure that's the way to achieve the duality we're talking about.

Communicating with your mate about your needs for both time together and time apart is crucial. Using your skills with I-messages, you can do this. Couples do something really nutty that I see with how they're going to spend their time: they focus on the doing rather than the being together — form over function. Time together can certainly take many forms.

Just being "proximal" is one way to spend time together, similar to "parallel play" as the child developmentalists would describe. You're in the kitchen wondering about new life forms emerging from the fridge while he's out edging the lawn or tinkering in the garage. And there's a comfort in that kind of time though it's not "knee to knee" connecting time. It counts. Proximal time registers on my meter.

Back to the form over function issue. A complaint I hear over and over is a variation of this: "We just don't like to do the same things." How about being together? You

liked being together well enough to get married, to be together for the rest of your days. So at some time you liked
being together. What were you doing then that you liked
so much? Since most of us marry in the midst of courtship (see opening chapter) we're still so enamored with
one another, we'd do anything to be in each other's company. While we were courting, I would go watch my sweetie
clean his tackle box, something I'd not want to do now.

In conceptualizing "time in a marriage," start thinking
about what you're really fussing about when you're fussing with your spouse about time. If it's about quantity,
you might be feeling unimportant and excluded. If you'll
think back to when you and your spouse were dating/
courting, you will likely recall how much time you spent
together.

Actually, time commitment is one of the earliest indi-
cations that the relationship is becoming serious. As you
include each other in your individual lives through sharing time together, the bond between you strengthens. As
you share time, you share experiences in that time and
this also strengthens the growing connection between you.
If you ask your new date to go to a family reunion that
represents a more serious commitment than if you ask
him/her to go to brunch on Sunday. Duality then is a factor — what you do with the time you have together.

The passage of time is the instrumental component
for all developmental processes and how you manage it
will directly affect the outcome. For example, if you plant
tomato seeds in your garden instead of going to the movie,
you will increase the probability of having tomatoes to eat.
The quality aspect then has to do with how you spend the
hours you have together. Not that you need to plant tomatoes, although when you're first dating and falling in love,
planting tomatoes can be fascinating; ergo, the cleaning
the tacklebox memory.

Our need for time with or without our partner is complicated by our emotional and physical condition. For example, when my father died four years ago, I needed the aforementioned "proximal time." I wanted Don close by even if I didn't feel like interacting much. His presence was a comfort. A wife told me in the office one time that she "enjoyed him (her husband) just puttering around in the garage because he was giving some energy to the household instead of to his golfing buddies."

Included in the concept of "proximal time" are joint projects, solo projects and parallel play. This is time together that is valuable because it represents and/or validates the existence of your coupleness. Most any task I am doing is somehow easier if Don is involved either directly or indirectly. I've heard this many times during the years, this need for proximal time. It is time shared that has meaning for your relationship.

Quality has to do with emotional intimacy that in my judgment is related somewhat to the quantity aspect. You can certainly connect with each other in an instant but not without the instant itself. Couples can endure lots of time deprivation but it will lead to emotional distance, which cannot usually be eliminated quickly.

Each of us has some expectations about how much time "we" should spend together as a married couple. And these generally come from our FOO and how our parents utilized time together. Let me tell you about Fred and Sally who came into the office right after Sally had announced she was ready to leave the marriage. She felt lonely, unimportant, and had become attracted to a man in her department at work who "takes the time to listen to me." There had not been a sexual affair but certainly an emotional affair was blooming.

Sally is an independent, self-reliant woman who came from a close knit family with a stay-at-home mother and a father who had no personal hobbies or leisure activities. The family enjoyed a lot of time together even when the children (Sally and her two brothers) began to migrate into the larger world. Time with the family was a top priority and moving into peer relationships was probably inhibited by this parental imperative. Sally came into her marriage expecting to spend a great deal of "discretionary" time with Fred who came from a family who operated very differently around time issues.

For one thing, Fred was an avid golfer and duck hunter, which here in Arkansas means you live in the duck blinds from November through January and golf season is any pretty day. Fred's dad took him and his brother hunting and/or golfing whichever the weather permitted, and Mom kept the home fires burning with a younger daughter. Fred was used to a lot of male companionship and didn't know quite what to do with Sally who didn't hunt or golf. She liked to shop and to look for "home gracers," Fred's term for objects that would "grace your fine home beautifully." He liked her choices for "gracers," so was content to hit the golf ball while she graced their home.

But Sally wasn't content. She wanted his participation in furnishing their home and Fred's lack of interest felt like a personal rejection.

Their dilemma was helped by "reframing," which is altering the spin you've put on something. Fred and Sally were focusing on the activity rather than the togetherness, thus choosing form over function. When my husband asks, "Do you want to go fishing?" I might say "no" but when he says, "I want you to go to the lake with me. Will you?" I say, "Yes." The invitation is about being together which might be just proximal time or it might turn into quality emotional intimacy time.

Fred and Sally tilted their view and began to focus on having fun together wherever. The being together took priority over the doing. Their refocus on function over form has helped them both enjoy new experiences. Fred is learning a lot about antiques and Sally now knows what a birdie is. Both have talked with each other about their time needs and though there are discrepancies, the two of them are working through them a day at a time.

I certainly encourage individual time for each spouse. Getting married doesn't strip you of your right to be an individual. In fact, the more individuality you can retain the better relationship you will have. You don't have to give up half yourself to make a whole with your partner's leftover half. Both of you get to stay whole and learn how to be together under those conditions.

Recently in the office, a couple in conflict over time issues brought up another time issue I need to address briefly: being "on time." This woman, married for 18 years, long ago had given up on her husband honoring time commitments to her. While she felt discounted and unimportant to him by his behavior, he had never been able to understand why she felt that way. A man with major issues of control, he would not respond to a time demand, though he never missed a tee time. He, however, set that appointment himself.

When folks have control issues, they are funny about time deadlines. The conventional wisdom in the office is that obsessives are right on time; passive-aggressives come late; anxiety disorders are always early.

You can learn something about yourself and your partner by being aware of how you handle time. My husband can stretch more seconds into 10 minutes than I can. Of course, time increments of less than 15 minutes don't exist for me. Being slightly OCD (obsessive-compulsive disorder), I am on time. I don't flirt with the all too rigid limitations of time. My spouse loves to live dangerously and fully expects time to expand whenever he needs extra minutes. Considering car trouble on the way to the airport would never cross his mind. That's one reason I married him. I knew I could learn new methods of living!

Oh, back to the couple. She has quit attaching painful meaning to his tardiness. "It's his deal," she declares sincerely. And she takes her own car now. No more struggles for her.

One more time issue couples need to address is about "timing." Choosing the moment "of occurrence so as to produce the most effective results," says Webster and that's pretty much what I want you to know about timing. I would never ask my spouse to fix anything if he's hungry unless I'm interested in some strife. And he knows not to require decisions or information from me after 6:15 on weeknights. Catch me in the a.m. when I'm rested and ready.

Watching and listening to your partner gives you crucial information about when he/she is most likely to respond in the manner you seek.

Most of you are too bright to falter in this area, but I did have a rather unaware young husband be disappointed when his wife was not sexually responsive after a root canal. "I forgot about your appointment," he said. She did not believe him.

Now to money and marriage: a sticky wicket if ever there was one. My belief forged by years of experience in my office with hundreds of married couples (and couples just "living together") is that all — yes, ALL couples have issues over money and more often than not these turn into conflicts between partners. The spouses have conflict because they don't know how to deal with settling their disputes about money: Whose money is it? How do we spend it? Who decides when, where, what, why, and how much? They have difficulty making decisions because:

1. *They don't openly talk about them.*
2. *They don't know how they each individually feel about money.*
3. *They don't understand the issues underlying the conflict.*

4. *They are not aware of FOO influences.*
5. *They are fearful of conflict (see Chapter 6)*
6. *Many people feel it's impolite to talk about money.*
   (I am not kidding.)

Money conflicts generally are about power and control. This is one area of the marital relationship that directly forces the couple to look at the power balance in their marriage. This balance is about the dollars and also about the attitudes and feelings each spouse brings into the marriage about money.

What does money represent to each of you? For most of us, money represents security and control. We want the means to make choices (security) and the ability to exercise them (control).

It's necessary for each of you to be aware of what money means to you and how you function because of these beliefs. You've got to be honest with yourself and confront yourself even if you don't think you ought to think or feel about money like you do.

I saw this really obnoxious man years ago when he was brought in by his long-suffering wife, heel marks all the way from the parking lot, and he told me about his "'Golden Rule' — He who makes the gold, rules." He meant it. His spouse had to ask him for every dime she spent and it was a degrading experience for her. In the beginning of their marriage, their joint decision had been that her "job" would be to run the house and to raise the children, worthy endeavors but not valued by her husband because she didn't produce dollars. Her solution was to use her education and get a job so she would have some say-so about money.

I was proud of her. By the way, he was terribly threatened by her ability to produce money and eventually had to come to marital therapy to work through the change in the power balance.

Couples get pretty sneaky about how they spend money since they won't talk about it. "Domestic money laundering" was a covert operation used by a housewife I saw to be able to wear the clothes she wanted. She devised bogus household expenses that seemed legitimate for extra cash and also used the kids as a source of income for her personal needs. She reported to me with a smile that her husband had remarked with a sigh one evening that "it costs me more to send these kids to public school than private with all these extra supplies I have to buy." The "supplies" were designer shoes for his wife and he didn't have a clue. She was good, a real pro.

Men get sneaky, too. A male patient of mine kept a new boat motor under his front porch for months before installing it because he was afraid his wife would disapprove and give him a lecture on the frivolity of his purchase. Both he and his wife worked, but their system (see below) was an "ours" structure which meant any personal expenditures had to be submitted for approval prior to purchase.

Most couples do try to set up some structure on how to deal with money issues so they don't really have to deal with money issues. Common systems established for Double Income couples:

1. *Mine, Yours, Ours*
2. *Mine and Yours*
3. *Mine and Ours*
4. *Yours and Ours*
5. *Ours*

For couples with one income producer common structures are:

1. *Ours*
2. *Mine*

3. Mine and ours.

Note: the conspicuous absence of any funds for "Yours."

Go back through the possibilities and read them aloud, alone at first and then with your partner. Each of you needs to hear your partner say the words. This is how it sounds: My Money, Your Money, and Our Money, My Money, Your Money. Mine. Yours. Money, money, money. Say it. Deal with your feelings about money. Get used to the concept of MONEY and who makes it and who says how it's going to be spent. This is a part of your marriage that has to be dealt with or you will end up hiding boat motors and stashing new clothes in grocery sacks underneath loaves of bread. What system have you and your spouse utilized? Did you talk about it? Do you like the way it works for YOU? Does the system feel "fair?"

The system that seems to work the best is the "Mine, Yours, and Ours" even if there is only one spouse receiving a W-2. With this structure, both partners are recognized as equals and have access to some personal discretionary funds. We don't like to feel childish and money issues with our partner can trigger that unpleasant situation.

Having to ask for money from a partner or to justify why you spent money to an inquiring mate can produce such feelings. I think each partner needs some "private" money if possible to avoid that situation. I hear over and over from stay-at-home spouses how miserable it is to not have money for lunch or a cart fee or a manicure and be fearful of asking. It's demeaning. You and your partner would be wise to discuss the issue of some personal funds each of you has that you can spend without explanation.

With the "ours" part of the arrangement, I encourage couples to set what I call the "Doodad" limit. How much can you spend before it requires joint approval? For some lucky couples, the doodad limit can be in the thousands. For most, it seems to be in the hundreds . . . or a hundred. One young couple I saw in their first year of marriage, both of them in school and working, had a $10 limit excluding groceries. It worked for them.

I also encourage couples who fight over money to sit down and pay the monthly bills together. It seems in most marriages, that one partner handles the finances. Perhaps, the spouses alternate taking that responsibility but more often than not (remember the selection process?) one will end up as financial manager, often an unappreciated and much maligned role. Soon this partner finds himself/herself setting limits with the other who usually resents such limits. Arguments are likely with accusations leveled of free spending or hoarding. Usually sitting down with the checkbook and the stack of bills to be paid will help the financial manager as well as the unaware spouse see the reality of the financial picture.

Really, the selection process often makes me believe in the wisdom and sense of humor of a Higher Power. Too many times for it to be just coincidence, I see the pairing of the frugal saver who thinks about the future and would never miss an insurance premium with the free-spending hedonist who lives for the moment and questions the usefulness of an IRA, much less a disability policy. Somehow these two find each other and soon begin what can be a lifelong struggle to manage their finances. And maybe their discovery of each other helps the species survive in the sense that the "little red hen" partner makes certain that the bread gets on the table for the family. "Little red hens" often attach to those who thrive for immediate gratification and if their struggle doesn't destroy them, a strong family unit will emerge.

What helps is a recognition and acknowledgment of their differences and negotiation of policy. This can happen if the "bad-good, right-wrong" mind-set gives over to that concept of "we're just different." Returning to that mind set again and again will help you bypass painful arguments.

"Marriage with peace is this world's Paradise;
With strife, this life's Purgatory."
—Unknown, Politeuphuia (1669)

Chapter 6

Conflicts and Confrontation

Couples often seem apologetic about having conflict as if this indicates some ominous weakness in the relationship. They can also be defensive about their conflicts, preferring to disown them and/or to attribute them to some other cause rather than to personal differences. This gives them distance from the emotional repercussions of the conflict but also encourages not accepting responsibility, which could lead to resolution.

I frequently reassure them that conflict is normal, appropriate, and that without it, "your marriage will die on the vine." I am not impressed, I am horrified when I hear spouses brag that they've never had a fight, an argument or even a disagreement! There is no way to live with another human being, sharing life's most precious resources (time, space, and money) without having SOME conflict. What's the big deal about conflict? What is so bad about confrontation?

Most of us fear conflict and confrontation because of the negative outcomes possible. We fear an argument (no yelling or cursing) or a fight (yelling and generic cussing, no name-calling or insults) because it can separate us from our spouse or produce disapproval from our mate which is anxiety producing. Arguing and "fighting" are like guns . . . they won't kill you, but the people having them can. Learning how to express your feelings whether they differ or not is your most important task if you want your partner to know you. And while similarities attract, it is likely that in resolving your differences, you become more intimate.

It is necessary that YOU have an attitude shift before we proceed. The shift is to accepting cognitively and emotionally that it's okay to have conflict with your spouse. I didn't say you had to like it, but you do need to accept it as a normal and okay part of marriage.

When couples are in disagreements they are confronted with their differences. Being different from each other often causes great anxiety especially in couples who are "enmeshed" into a big old "WE-US" blob that is so encumbering it prevents individuality. Getting married is not "two becoming one" which would be deadly to each spouse's personal being but more "one becoming two" as spouses learn to accommodate to a whole other person with whom they share life. There are powerful psychodynamic processes at work when we select a mate and emotionally relate to that mate.

By encouraging couples to confront and participate in conflict and its resolution, I am encouraging them to individuate. The position is "I stay me and you stay you even if we're married and we work toward accepting and understanding each other. We will not try to stamp-out traits in each other that cause us to be different but to respect them even when they cause us anxiety."

Okay, now that you're into your attitude shift, let's take a look at how you might deal with resolving conflict so that each of you emerges from the experience intact and undamaged. Many of the couples who come in for treatment are fearful and avoidant of conflict and the need to confront. If you're avoiding conflict, you're also avoiding intimacy because you can't be close to someone with whom you aren't willing to share your feelings.

The way you express your feelings is, of course, crucial. It reminds me of an older man I saw my first year in practice who began every session saying he wasn't going to come back because "none of this is helping me. People are still too stupid to understand me." Well, this man finally "got it." He came to his session one day, all smiles, eager to share an experience he had had at his small town Rotary Club meeting. "You know, Rebecca, there is a big difference in telling someone 'I don't agree with you,' instead of 'You're full of _____!'"

Bingo! His life improved dramatically as did his marriage.

How do you deal with your feelings? Are you an Internal Processor (IP) or an External Processor (EP)? Those who figure out what their feelings are over time before they speak are IP's and those who start speaking before they've processed their emotions and do it right before your very eyes are EP's.

My very own husband is an IP who has it all down pat before I get to know anything, which used to drive me nuts. "Are you in there? Squeeze my hand if you hear me," I'd say, frustrated because I couldn't tell what he was feeling. Early in our marriage, when he got mad, he'd just walk out of the house, into the garage, get into his car and drive away. The time he spent away was directly related to how many confusing emotions he had to work through before he could speak.

One July 4th, he stayed gone for 12 hours, a recess I deemed a little excessive. When he returned, I was so mad I didn't care what he felt. We've improved a lot over the years, i.e., he only walks into another room and I've learned to keep my mouth shut until he's ready to talk. He still works it out internally but he often lets me know where he is in the process. "Precincts reporting," but it's better than nothing.

I, on the other hand, need to rattle off all the emotional data no matter how trivial in front of him and work it out, "Out There." I sort of throw everything on some canvas I can see and after all the splats have hit, I begin to piece it together, moving toward some coherent emotional place. It used to scare him to death but he's learned this is how I do it and that what I'm saying at any given moment is just the means, not always the "end."

Often IP's and EP's have difficulty initially since they process emotional responses so differently. Knowing how you and your partner get to the emotional sharing place is useful. Either method is fine; one is not better or worse than the other. Identifying how you both function in processing and sharing your feelings needs to be done so the two of you can collaborate (see Chapter 8) in this all important issue.

Here is a "pearl": it's okay to go to bed angry. Conflict cannot always get fixed on demand. Sometimes you just have to tolerate the discomfort and anxiety until you can find a resolution. Do not demand that you or your partner "get over it" until he/she has.

Today in my office, right in the middle of my writing this chapter, Greg and Kathy were in for their eighth session. They both were complaining that "we're just spinning our wheels." I asked each of them to extract himself/ herself from the "we-glob" and say how "I've been spinning MY wheels." What emerged was blame. Each blamed the other for the lack of progress they've made during this separation that is now close to six months.

Married for about 10 years, the last four or five have been very unsatisfying for Greg who believes he was letting Kathy know of his unhappiness. Kathy says she does not remember any direct communication from him about his misery, which is mainly around lack of sexual contact.

They have three children, which have taken top priority since they were born, and both Greg and Kathy work full, time consuming jobs.

Where was time for each other? Where was time to talk, to share, to enjoy the attention and understanding of their mate? Didn't happen and here they are, years away from the initial problem that they failed to confront and deal with. Now they want to blame the other for how they got here.

If you're blaming your partner, you're not accepting personal responsibility for the state of your marriage. You will make progress when you're willing to confront yourself and what you did or didn't do that promoted this crisis in your marriage.

Blaming won't help, I promise. Greg and Kathy listened to me, and neither said a word for maybe five minutes — a long time in silence.

Greg started: "I did not tell you clearly how I was feeling especially about your lack of sexual interest in me because I was afraid of how you'd react. I know I need to be able to talk about what I'm feeling more than I do."

Kathy then accepted responsibility for leaving him and their couple time in a low-priority spot while she advanced at work and spent any extra time with the children. The wheels began to quit spinning. I'm not sure what will happen at this point but I do know they have a better chance now than they did when denying personal responsibility. If you're blaming someone else for where you are, you will lose yourself. Trust me. Another pearl.

Avoiding "hot" topics are what most couples do, rationalizing in all kinds of ways why they need to keep quiet. Common rationalizations are:

1. *It's not THAT important.*
2. *He/she won't understand.*

3. *He/she will get angry.*
4. *It's not worth the effort.*
5. *I want to watch "ER."*
6. *I don't want to ruin the evening, the day, the week-end.*

Of course, later when the original unexpressed feelings have been buried under more unexpressed feelings, things emotionally begin to get confusing. That's why so often when a fight erupts, you find yourself in a morass of old resentments and hurts that are tumbling out in a litany that your partner will shield himself/herself from fairly quickly, and then begin what is usually a strong defensive maneuver, and the derailment has occurred. End of hope for THIS attempt at "clearing the air." It's more like bombs bursting than smoke evaporating.

While all the excuses may feel valid, what you're really doing in avoiding confrontation/conflict is to foster a sense of your own dependency on the approval of your partner which will lead to resentment. "Bite the hand that feeds me" type resentment. But the most damaging aspect of not dealing with your differentness from your partner is to not let your partner know you. Your refusal to risk showing who you are by owning and expressing your feelings denies personal growth for yourself and prevents your spouse from knowing who you are. If anyone is going to have that privilege, it is your marriage partner.

Couples who are prone to avoid possible dissension will have an elaborate and unspoken system of communicating only about those safe subjects. They get held hostage by their partner's possible reaction, which is often anger and/or disapproval and surprisingly, anxiety. Many couples have an unspoken collusion around anxiety: "You don't do anything to make me anxious (like disagree with me, criticize me, or do something I don't want you to do) and I won't do anything to make YOU anxious." These couples may be able to carry this off for the short term but over a lifetime, who would want this? "I won't grow because you might become anxious and you mustn't grow because I don't want to feel anxious." Think about it.

Let me tell you about Martha who never would drive on the interstate with her two small children because Chuck could not tolerate worrying about his family being on the road in a car that could be in an accident. Thus, for well over eight years, Martha stayed put . . . or her parents drove the hour-and-one-half to come get her and the children. While she resented the control Chuck was exercising over her activities, she didn't want him to be miserable while she went where she wanted to go. Finally, several months into therapy she told him solemnly and directly, "Chuck, I resent your asking me to change my behavior so YOU won't have to feel anxious. I am going to drive to see my parents when I need and want to and you will have to handle yourself." Though he escalated with symptoms like acid stomach and severe headaches, Martha held her ground. Chuck had a choice: grow or go. He stayed and Martha drove and their marriage took a step toward health.

Once you know what you are feeling and what you want to share with your partner then you do it. Go back to the communication chapter and refresh your skills in using clear "I" statements. When you're talking about yourself, you are the expert. No one SHOULD challenge your statements of your feelings and YOU SHOULD NOT challenge your partner either. Allow yourself to be different and accept the differences in your spouse. I know that if you're reading this book, you've got good verbal skills.

Again, conflict resolution is made less threatening when:

1. *You accept that conflict is normal.*
2. *You accept that being different from each other does*

not mean you should divorce.
3. *You accept that sometimes the only solution to con-flict is to compromise.*

Compromise is a situation in which each of you gets some of what is desired. Remember you're adults, you're mature, and you can't have both cookies. You trust your-self to hang on and work through whatever needs to be worked through. Compromise is not copping out. It re-quires a lot of patience and maturity to achieve.

"Maturity: When we can treat ourselves in our own way rather than within the automatic ways of our parents in childhood."
—Hugh Missildine

Chapter 7

Requests, Demands and Making the Deal

Marty and Ruth came in on a Monday morning after a weekend drive through the Arkansas Ozarks. Ordinarily seeing the Ozarks in October can cure a cold but Marty and Ruth needed more than scenery to ease the ache of chronic marital conflict.

From their appearance in the waiting room, I knew things had not gone well. Their body language broadcast their misery. They were sitting on opposite ends of the sofa, legs crossed outward, practically back to back while sitting side by side, a familiar marital stance for this middle-aged couple in a five-year-old second marriage. I solemnly led them down the hall, wondering who was the injured party. They often competed for the position.

It was Ruth who began talking the second the door closed, eager to tell me how badly Marty had behaved and how poorly he had treated her on their mini-getaway. She was wounded, but so was Marty who was confused as well.

"I stopped at every antique shop in five counties. I even offered to pull over if I saw a pile of junk by the side of the road," he said.

"But," Ruthie wailed, "you didn't want to." Marty looked

at me, eyes upward, a resigned silence.

Clearly Ruth was not up to accepting "willing to" from a partner who couldn't give her "want to." Since we're not in charge of our "want to's," sometimes willing is all we can offer.

I wonder often how many unseen movies, uneaten pizzas, hurt feelings, wasted time, and other missed adventures have resulted from an inability to accept a partner's position of "I don't want to, but I'm willing." This is one of the most frequent snags seen in my office.

"Do you want to go to a movie?" he asks.

"No," she says, "but I will."

"Oh, just forget it. We won't go." He couldn't accept her willingness, which should be good enough.

I think the snags happen because of the amount of emotional risk involved. I don't see couples having trouble with the "willing-want to" component when one asks the other, "Will you take out the garbage?" or "Do you want to pick up the cleaning?" These chore/task requests are fundamentally different from those requests that involve asking your partner to give you something personal, like time or attention.

I repeat the quote from Chapter Five: "Time is the currency of love. Don't tell me how much you love me; how much time are you going to spend with me?" (I talk about this more in Chapter 6. I read this years' ago and know it to be true and wish I'd said it. Had I known more then, I would have.) So the kind of transactions I 'm talking about here are those that have the emotional element involved, albeit implied, it's there: "If you love me, you'll do this for me."

Down deep we all at times adhere to "the myth of Mother love" which is, "If you loved me, I wouldn't even have to ask. You'd know my needs and wants and attend to them promptly, joyfully, and unbidden."

Wrong.

Anyway, here are four request transactions that you need to know about and be able to recognize. Being able to utilize them will help your relationship run more smoothly: The first is a **Gift,** the second a **Sacrifice,** the third is a **Business Deal,** and the fourth is a **Growth Opportunity.** Also, these are written as requests FROM your partner but work just the same when you're the asking party.*

1. *Your partner asks you for something you can give freely. There is no charge. This is a freebie, a **gift.***
2. *Your partner asks you for something you can't give freely but you're willing to accommodate, to make a **sacrifice,** if you will. There is a charge, but it's all yours. YOU CANNOT PUNISH YOUR PARTNER NOW OR EVER FOR YOUR CHOICE TO ACCOMMODATE.*
3. *Your partner asks you for something you can't give freely and aren't willing to accommodate unless you get something back. There is a charge and you've got to let your partner know on the front end what that charge is. This is a **Business Deal.***

"Okay, I'll go to your uncle's (whom I've only met twice and both times he called me the wrong name, and was blisteringly boring,) 80th birthday party if you'll go to that office picnic with me." This is a simple transaction if the terms of the deal are clearly set out in the beginning. This is a *"business deal."*

This transaction, the trade-off or business deal is tricky. Sometimes the spouse agreeing to the request will make a "silent deal" meaning he/she will know what the charge is but won't reveal it until later. It goes like this: "What do you mean you won't go to my parents for Thanksgiving? I went to your folks last year." So the unsuspect-

---

* *I'm not sure where I first learned about these types of transactions but I've used the original concept and added to and modified them through the years.*

ing spouse gets a bill he didn't know he owed, an IOU he never signed. It is crucial to let the asking spouse know the deal so he/she will be making an informed choice. This is not an opportunity for manipulation or being sneaky.

4. Growth Opportunity: You don't want to and aren't willing to. This last one is a difficult transaction and a valid one. Your partner asks for something that you cannot and will not be able to give or accommodate. It's non-negotiable. You have no price. (I've seen this one in the sexual arena when one partner wants an activity the other finds unacceptable.) The emotional position is "I don't want to and I am not willing to." There are times this is the situation and there is no changing it, i.e., your partner cannot or will not budge.

And remember, there will be times when this is you in the "can't-won't" position. Negotiating is out, compromise is not possible so what do you have left? An acceptance of your partner's position, like it or not. I have worked with couples unable to tolerate this blatant "separatism," this outrageous refusal by a spouse to comply with a need/want expressed. What happens is the partner being "denied" in some way, will escalate coercion tactics, bringing manipulation to a new level art form but still meeting their partner's firm refusal to give in.

This is the "growth opportunity" mentioned above. Now you can suck it up, take a deep breath, and calm and soothe yourself. You must be careful not to attach negative meaning, i.e., "This person does not care about me much less love me enough to be married to me." Don't do that to you, your spouse, or your relationship. When we marry, remember, the license is to marry, it's not a license that entitles us to perfect attunement with this other human being from another gene pool.

Let me address the "requisition" part of this chapter. Requisition is a nice word for "demand." There are times when marital partners will make a demand of their spouse.

A demand is different from a request which by its nature implies an acceptance of the partner's right of refusal. By making a demand, a requisition, the demanding partner is saying, " I cannot accept a refusal. I must have what I'm asking for." Of course, demands are legitimate at times but I strongly advise each of you to use them prudently.

Common demand/requisition areas are usually around time, money and sex issues. It is helpful if you're going to make a demand of your partner, that you clearly state that what you're asking for is just that. Good luck with these. They are tricky and should be used rarely. And not for trivialities.

Knowing the dynamics of these common interactions really seems to help the couples I've seen. The awareness legitimizes or gives permission for each partner to have not only opposing feelings from the partner but also the right of refusal. Accepting your own feelings when they differ from your partner and your right to choose based on your feelings is being mature and once again, good marriages are made up of mature people or people trying to be.

*"Demands are tricky and should be used rarely
— and not for trivialities."*
—R. Ward

Chapter 8

Collaboration

Some years ago, I noticed that I was using the word "collaborate" frequently in couple sessions. "You need to collaborate on this," or "Being more collaborative would help here," and "If you could collaborate with each other on this, you would reduce your tension." Over and over, I heard myself speak of "being collaborative" and/or working toward a "more collaborative spirit" in the relationship. Over time I saw couples develop some of this collaborative spirit and then I observed that their conflicts would both reach resolution more quickly and actually diminish over time. I decided I was on to something here with this collaboration idea and continued to use the concept because it worked.

I did look up the word in the dictionary to see if I were using it correctly and was pleased at what I found. The first most common meaning of the word collaborate was "to work together." Well, that's what I was meaning when I used the word as a directive with couples. The second meaning in the dictionary was "to cooperate with an enemy invader." That too seemed to fit perfectly! I'll make the point that collaborating with your partner can keep him or her from becoming your enemy.

Often when couples wait too long to come into therapy, they can feel like enemies to each other, perceiving the partner as "out to get me." These couples are miserable. They are usually easy to recognize and my receptionist is an expert. She hands me their intake, rolls her eyes, and says, "Hope you ate your Wheaties." The bitterness and hostility ooze from them like swamp gas. They are weary, wary, and almost hopeless. (The truly hopeless go to attorneys, not therapists.)

These couples are difficult to be around. They have let issues go unresolved for years along with unspoken feelings that have lay fermenting ready to explode at any time. Attributions and assumptions, all negative and hostile, are prevalent. Interpretations are almost always inaccurate and always inflammatory. Communication is treacherous and they know it, so they tread into any interaction tentatively unless they're ready for an all out verbal melee. I can sit and watch the couple attempt to talk to each other and marvel at how this English speaking couple has managed to turn their common language into a multilingual crapshoot. He says "a-b-c;" she hears "m-n-o," replies "w-r-t." He is confused, blames her for the mistranslation, and as she is running into their language barrier she gives up by retreat or retort.

The language barrier is the countless unspoken feelings and unresolved issues that have grown-up between them providing enough snarls and tangles to make any attempt to get through them treacherous at best. For these couples communication is hopeless and they know it. They fear the bad feelings that most any interaction generates so they continue to avoid communicating unless it's imperative. Then they usually do a "hit and run" type deal that gets the information across without risking any true attempt at connecting. "I smell smoke. There may be a fire. Run."

Now they are in my office wondering what in the world I'll be able to do to help in one hour. Sometimes I wonder, too. At some level, they know it has taken them a long time to get themselves into this mess and suspect it will take time to resolve but they are in such pain, they want relief immediately. I understand. A bad, mad marriage is a painful thing. I tell them I am going to be, among other things, an interpreter for them until they speak a common tongue and learn to collaborate.

Will and Lucille are a good example of a couple who learned to collaborate. They had been married about 30 years when I first saw them and they should have come in 27 years earlier. They lived in a small town some hours away where he ran a successful business that Lucy helped with occasionally. An unadmitted workaholic, Will was an "alpha dog" at work all day and had difficulty giving up that role at home. He was demanding and critical, traits he described in his father but failed to acknowledge in himself.

She mainly stayed home and kept a perfect house. By nature, Lucy was driven by obsessive-compulsive traits but they weren't severe enough to make her dysfunctional or require medication, but were just enough to promote hyper-organization and cleanliness in the home.

Their biggest problem was around time and perfection. She could never be on time, which was important to Will, and he wouldn't respond to her need for an uncluttered house. She used to describe Will's coming home in the evening like this: "He's like a dump truck. He walks through the door and the house begins to look like a landfill area. How can one man make so much litter?" During the years, rather than look at how to work these issues through, they had just gotten more and more frustrated.

First Will and Lucille had to move past the fantasy of being able to change their partner's personality to a more desirable and compatible one and to accept the reality of the personality they had married. We all have to get to this point. Along with this acceptance, there needs to be the piece that allows understanding rather than suspicion that the spouse only is the way he/she is for spite. We don't get married and become different people. We bring to marriage what we are and it, like developing fluid for film, promotes the emergence of our traits.

Avoid blaming your partner for your gene pool, your family of origin, and your childhood influences. How many times have I heard in the office an angry spouse accuse the partner of causing his/her behavior. "I wouldn't act like this if it weren't for you." You must take responsibility for how you are because personality traits are implanted long before you learned your multiplication tables much less had your first date. Your partner is off the hook. Accept this!

So Will and Lucy extricated their own personal negative and positive traits from the relationship and began to see both themselves and their partner with this detachment, which promoted understanding.

As Will began to understand himself he could tell Lucy about himself and she was undergoing the same process. First there is the separation of self from the relationship. You extricate yourself so you can examine how you are as a separate being. Second, you gain awareness of how you function in the relationship, why you feel and act the way you do. Some questions to help you do this are these:

1. *What do I need and want?*
2. *How do I express these needs and wants?*
3. *How do I express my emotions in general?*
4. *Which emotions do I feel most often?*
5. *Do I take responsibility for my choices?*
6. *What are my "core" issues?*
7. *How do they affect my marriage?*

Core issues are those that keep popping up again and again for you to deal with such as issues around "fairness" or "consideration" or money. Usually you can spot yours by being aware of repetitive intense emotional reactions to stimuli that seem disproportionate. "Emotional overkill" is descriptive. They will be yours to learn about and as you do, you can better handle yourself in all relationships.

After you've accomplished this self-awareness through separation and examination, you then begin to let your partner in on your knowledge. You take the risk to let your spouse really know you, something we all need. I'm not talking about being able to predict behavior but about knowing how someone IS inside. And now you can find out what marriage can really be.

In a healthy, collaborative marriage YOUR PARTNER WILL HELP YOU DEAL WITH YOURSELF. When you discover some of your own "stuff" or craziness and share that with your partner, you now have someone to help you out from time to time when you really need it.

Will began to understand his drive to succeed and how it affected his marriage. His often-unrealistic expectations of his own performance leaked out into the same unrealistic expectations of Lucy, which caused him to be critical of her.

Lucy already was dealing with strong perfectionist needs herself, so any criticism coming from the outside was just about too much. She would become more rigid, more controlling and obsess about the house staying immaculately clean. They each began to talk to each other about what they were feeling rather than act it out, certainly a developmental step toward maturity.

I tell couples over and over, "Say what you're feeling." There's a big difference in telling your spouse, "I'm so mad I could hit you," and actually hitting him/her. Being able to talk about what is happening inside of you to your partner will help you process your emotions and will help your partner understand what is happening to you so he/she can help you.

As Will became in touch with how his drives were causing him to be critical of Lucy, he became less so and took care of his frustrations in more healthy ways. He started exercising and decided to put some energy into the yard. He also quit struggling with Lucy about time. They agreed if she was running late, whatever the reason, he would take his vehicle and she would come when she was ready. Will understood that sometimes Lucy's need to control her comings and goings was going to kick-in and there was no need to attach a negative or personal meaning to it. "That's just Lucy," he came to accept.

Will and Lucy arrived at a collaborative spirit in their marriage and after 30-plus years, they enjoyed their marriage more than they ever had before. They began to dance rather than wrestle. They began to really know each other and to help each other deal with those little crazies that each of us have.

For example: I am a little crazy about air travel. Since I don't much trust airlines to have the plane they promised or my seat on it reserved, I want to be at the gate about an hour before departure. My husband would like to leap onto the plane as it backs away from the tunnel, so we had some conflict earlier in our marriage. He tried for a long time to "talk" me out of my anxiety using logic and reason to prove my "silliness." He even tried shaming me into behaving more rationally. Anxiety is often resistant to spousal discounting so we had to find a better way.

Collaboration was our answer. He began to understand that my anxiety was not something I was manufacturing to irritate him or to control him but was about me and time and being left and on and on. We talked and he heard my angst about something I didn't understand so well myself. He reframed — put a new spin on the situation —

and used the extra time to read or people watch or visit with me since he wasn't mad at me anymore. I don't think he understands in the purest sense why I become anxious but he accepts me and my craziness and that feels really good.

Maybe collaboration has to do with being able to accept each other's craziness and helping one another deal with it. Marriage is certainly about the best place I know to get some help with yourself. Once you get past struggling and more into collaborating, here is a relationship that allows you to be a little neurotic, a little infantile from time to time, and certainly, true to self.

Just this week, I saw a young couple, James and Diana, who are just getting ready to learn about all of this. Married just two years, they came in because they had a fight and James shouted, "I can't live with this. I want a divorce."

The "D-word" stopped the fight immediately and scared them both, as commitment to marriage is important to each. Their fight was over money, in particular how Diana was spending too much according to James.

They each spoke their piece, agreed they were poles apart in their attitudes and spending habits, and then as if they had emptied a huge jigsaw puzzle in my lap, said, "Now, what? We're totally different and don't see a solution."

"You'll have to learn to understand each other and collaborate about this issue," I said. "It's going to take work." They sighed and looked glum. "You're not on a date here, folks, you're married. Welcome to reality."

Diana said, "But I didn't think this kind of stuff started until about the seventh year!"

Wrong.

The time is now!

"Maturity is not the absence of conflict but knowing how to cope with it."
—Anonymous

In Closing

In the first few years after I started in the private practice of psychotherapy, my learning curve was steep and
often painful. While I was learning about the psychody-
namics of my patients and expanding my technical toolbox,
I was also learning about myself. I became acutely aware
of my own limitations as a healthy whole of a half of a
couple. I had heard often that I couldn't "take my patients
beyond my own growth." That scared me to death because
early on, I saw I was going to have to mature a great deal
to be able to be married the way I could be, should be, and
aspired to be. Luckily, I found I could take people beyond
my limitations with some "do as I say, not what I do" in-
struction but also because I was aware of those limitations
and I worked on them along with those of my patients. If
you know where to ford the streams, you can share that
information even if you've never actually gone across.

When I started graduate school in 1975, one of my
professors said that people go into psychology for three
reasons:

1. *Personal growth*

2. *Interest in people and the wish to help them, and*
3. *Voyeurism.*

I think he was right. The truth is, I have grown along with each of the people I've worked with through the years and I certainly hope they learned more from me than I from them. Or at the very least it was a draw. After all, none of them ever charged me for my education.

I saw a couple during those early years that I knew revealed a truth I would need to recall and respect ever after. Dean and Abby. They had been married about 15 years and were each about 40 when they came in. When I came out to get them, they sat across the room from each other in the waiting room, broadcasting their emotional distance and perhaps, level of frustration. After I introduced myself, they said they wanted to come in separately initially and might meet together later if I had time, so that's what we did. I wondered who had a secret.

Dean came in first and had a litany of complaints, one of which was about sex. "We never have sex," he reported. Later, when Abby came in, one of her complaints was "we have sex all the time." I thought this very interesting but what was even more interesting was while in for their joint session they AGREED that they had sex twice a week! His perception that twice a week was "never" and hers that it was "all the time" taught me the necessity of dealing with the perception of reality that each spouse will have. And this is a crucial lesson for spouses to integrate as well.

Your partner's perception is his/her reality, like it or not, and you need to:

1. *Let him/her tell you about it and*
2. *Listen when he/she does.*

Yes, I know that perception is not always reality but try telling that to someone who thinks it is. Each of you will have to accommodate to another person's view of life if you're married to them. You can tell a friend or family "You're wrong," but that won't work with your spouse.

You've read much of what I know about making marriage a healthy enjoyable relationship, a relationship that promotes you growing-up, not going crazy. And people in a bad marriage feel sort of crazy. Of course, most of them tend to think first, that it's really their partner who is nuts but eventually there comes a nagging suspicion that "I might be the crazy one." The way out of this disturbing development is to go back to blaming the partner. "I wouldn't act/feel/think/do/or be THIS way if you would act/feel/think/do/or be the way you're supposed to."

You'll do better knowing that feeling crazy is usually an omen that you're about to start another move toward maturity. Growing is painful and I've sure felt at times like I didn't want to do anymore of it for awhile.

Marriage is such a complicated relationship. Long before we ever meet our spouse, we've already been programmed by our Family of Origin on how we're going "to be" in the marriage. Our emotional wiring is in place and will kick-in under the intense emotional requirements of the marital relationship.

If you want to explore your own pre-programming, you will have to look backwards. This "revisiting" of your beginnings may be painful as well as enlightening and liberating and not everyone has the opportunity or inclination to take the trip. If you do, look at the marriage YOU were around during your childhood and adolescence and even now if your parents are still around and still married.

Their marriage is the prototype of your internal vision of marriage, a template if you will. Whether we consciously try to have a marriage different from our parents or one very similar, we are still greatly influenced by the way the marriage we grew up around was conducted. Return to the FOO chapter and look again at those questions. You're trying to get aware of the unconscious forces that may be hindering you in your goal toward a healthy marriage.

While I enjoy working with individuals and groups, working with couples is truly fascinating to me. They present innumerable puzzles to solve and intricacies of emotional transferences and contamination from the past to delve into for elucidation about what's happening in the present. So often "there and then" affect "here and now" and they don't know it. How exciting to see the "I get it" experience happen to someone who has been confused and miserable because he/she didn't "get it."

Many of these stand out in my memory for they are what keep me doing what I do with such enthusiasm, joy, and commitment. People can learn how to be married, remain individuals and absolutely not go crazy. Marriage can be a positive catalyst for personal growth and offer the best opportunity for intimacy. Real intimacy. The intimacy that comes from the risk taking spoken about throughout this book and in doing so, letting another person with his/her fragile chemical composition, become indispensable to you. A young physician beginning to experience this kind of connection with his wife of 11 years, tearfully said, "Rebecca, this is so scary. I can't imagine my life without her."

Before ending, let me tell you some interesting conundrums I've observed in working with couples. One of the most puzzling is that spouses promote the very thing they complain about.

For example, Marge brought a reluctant Henry into therapy complaining that he never shared his feelings with her, one of the most common complaints I hear. She went on and on about how "closed he is, never letting me know what's going on inside of him."

After several sessions, Henry did open up and tell Marge some of his feelings and it scared her to death. She completely over-reacted, becoming truly fearful as Henry revealed his vulnerability. He ended up comforting her, and looked at me sadly and said, "And this is why I don't talk to her."

Another puzzling thing couples do is reverse their attractions. I almost always ask the question, "What attracted you to your partner?" and then discover that this usually is what's driving them crazy now.

"Oh, she was so outgoing and friendly. She loved being with people and socializing," the husband replied. NOW he says she is "flirtatious and seductive and never wants to stay home."

The wife who was attracted by her husband's dependability now describes him as "rigid." A husband who was valued before marriage for being "laid back and untemperamental" now "lazy and irresponsible." Or a wife sought after for her competency and organization has now become "controlling." So watch what attracted you to your partner and know that you're normal when you now experience the flip side of the desirable trait you were so enamored with.

Couples generally get into trouble with expectations in the marriage. Some expectations we know about before we marry, some we don't.

I had no idea I had such "gender related chore expectations" until I heard myself pronounce one day "taking out the garbage is YOUR job."

Knowing about your unconscious expectations is just as necessary as knowing the conscious ones. We're always responsible for our behavior but we can only change it if we're aware of it.

Ignorance is no defense even in your marriage! Usually these unconscious ones are the ones that get us into trouble — because we are acting on them without awareness.

One of marriage's most painful characteristics is how our beloved can nail us on our unrealistic expectations as well as our undesirable personal habits and personality traits. H.L Menchen once said, "A man may be a fool and not know it but not if he's married." While we're striving toward emotional intimacy with our beloved spouse, he or she is also nailing US about how we "really are" and it's often very painful and will have an element of truth to it. If your partner says, even in a fit of anger, using the dreaded "You statement" that "You're inconsiderate" or "You only think about yourself," or "You're just like your brother" (who is an unemployed tattooed divorced felon), better give it some thought. Your partner won't be all right but he/she won't be all wrong either. While your first defensive response might be a version of *"Moi?"* or "Who ARE you talking about?" let it simmer and be open to the notion that a tad of what your spouse says, even in anger, will be true. Yuck. Here is that "marriage will grow you up" business at work.

This seems like the opportunity to add what I've observed about the issue of shopping in marriage. Wives often ask their husbands to go shopping with them. And most often husbands don't want to go. And don't, unless there is some indication that going might increase the chances of great sex later on. From what I've heard over the last 20 years, females like to shop and males don't like to shop. They like to buy. One husband described it thus: "I am a mission shopper. I know what I want, find out where it is, and go buy it. My wife can know what she wants, find it, and then she has to stalk it for awhile. Drives me crazy!" I think he summed it up nicely. Women like to go shopping; we like to "shop around." We may find something we want and/or need but we want to think about it awhile. Unless it's THE pair of shoes we've searched a lifetime for and then we'll snatch it up on the spot. But shopping is more than about purchasing for us. We're looking, we're thinking, we're dreaming. I'm not sure that we ought to expect our spouses to experience all that we do when we head out to the Mall or some wonderful specialty shop we've been touted on. We're off on an adventure. Usually our spouse will see it as an odious task and put a damper on our excitement. My advice would be to accept what may be a gender deal and not to attach any negative personal meaning to his reluctance or refusal to go with you. This is not a do-or-die issue but it appears so often as a point of conflict in the office that I wanted to include it. You are not alone.

Let me share this bit of wisdom with you before I go. Within your marriage, feelings are sacred, meaning you and your partner need to honor and respect each other's feelings even when you:

1. *Don't understand them.*
2. *Think they are ridiculous, silly, immature, unfair, impossible, illogical, or crazy.*
3. *Wish you'd married someone without the emotional component.*

I am often in the room when a couple will share a feeling that he/she has never taken the risk to share before, a feeling unspoken for years and years, and the power sharing has in bringing the couple closer is something to be able to see.

Recently a woman told her husband through tears and stammering how she had resented his sexual demands on her through the years and herself for meeting them and how this was affecting her feelings toward him. She had been clinically depressed, suicidal, and had done some destructive acting act, all efforts to avoid both her feelings and telling them to her husband.

Finally, after months of painful relating and withdrawal, she shared her feelings with him and for the first time in almost a year, smiled from relief and said, "I feel so close to you right this minute." This pair, married almost

30 years, is just now beginning to truly KNOW each other.

Each has become aware of himself/herself and how they function, taken responsibility for their feelings and behavior, and risked telling the partner. Self-awareness leads to acceptance of responsibility which promotes taking the risk to share with the partner.

When you've reached the powerful state of owning your "stuff" rather then blaming your parents or your partner and often in marriage we simply shift the blame, you're ready to risk. You're not dependent now on the response of your partner. You don't block taking the risk because you think your spouse will be disapproving, angry, disappointed, and so forth. You tell because you will feel close and that's what you want. The path to intimacy is simply this. The secret is out, the mystery solved.

There is more always to say on the mystery of marriage and how to have a happy, healthy one. Hopefully, you've learned in these few pages enough for you to begin to have what you want with your partner. Let me share one more crucial bit of advice an old mentor of mine told me years and years ago: "Don't mess with your partner's mouth." What he meant was don't tell your partner what to eat, what to drink, what to smoke, or how to talk.

He was right. People don't like to have their mouths interfered with. It's pretty primary and elementary stuff. Babies want something in their mouths when THEY want something in there but try putting anything in when they are not cooperative. Well, you and I are the same way. We don't want our mouths messed with. And I've certainly done just a little of that throughout the book and especially in the communication chapter. But more importantly I have tried to "mess with your minds" in a constructive, informative way. What I've presented here in these chapters are rock solid solutions to problems that some or all of the couples who come in to see me present. There are others to consider but these are the most prevalent.

Let me know if I succeeded messing with your minds in a constructive way. Your personal response is very important and I won't know how you feel unless you tell me.

"A person's character is but half formed till after wedlock."
—C. Simmons

Epilogue

Years ago I decided I would always have something to talk about with other women if I talked about childbirth. Women love to talk about birthing their babies. When my son was beginning to get a little hairy, I realized that boat had sailed and that it was way past time to "let it go" and move on to other communal topics. I settled on relationships. And then could talk to men as well. While childbirth certainly didn't invite much male conversation, relationships had more of a chance though men are more likely to enjoy "concrete" subjects, i.e., "How 'bout them Hogs?" Most of us like to talk about relationships because we are by our birthright relational creatures. It's in our cells. We are born needing people and all our lives we will need them, maybe in the purest sense, not to survive but to thrive. The problems we have in accepting and expressing this basic human need are myriad and complex and infinitely interesting to me. That fascination led me into my profession. And I love what I do. It truly "feeds my soul" as my son observed some years ago when he left banking to go into medical school. He said at that time that he wanted to do something every day that he could enjoy as much as I enjoyed my work.

Since I started in 1979 in an outpatient mental health center in my small Arkansas hometown, I have been in awe of the process of psychotherapy and counseling. (The difference in the two has to do with the level of intervention and focus in the sessions. Counseling is usually centered around problems and situations that the client recognizes and presents. Psychotherapy involves bringing into the client's awareness certain issues that might be interfering with successful life adjustment.) What I get to do every day is exciting even when it's boring because I get to relate to my patients on an intense emotional level. There is little "namby-pamby chit-chat" as one of my group members called it. There is work to be done by both me and the patient — complicated, often painful emotional work.

No matter who walks in for treatment, he/she brings others in as well. The room is filled with so many people even when there is only one person there. I've got Mom and Dad there plus grandparents and siblings, spouses and children, teachers and preachers . . . all the people who influenced the patient in my office. And when there is a couple in the room, it really gets crowded. Sorting through it all is tedious at times but almost always productive.

One of the first "exercises" I invite couples to do is this: each of you think about and write down how you contribute to the state of your marriage. Look at yourself as a marriage partner. What difficulties would you have being married to you. In any marriage, you get to take half the credit and half the blame. So after you've begun to recognize some of your own contributions, then write down what your partner brings to the problems. Generally couples come in hoping the problems they're having is the sole responsibility of the mate and find out very quickly it's their joint dynamics that have to be addressed. Folks that can accept this as reality will generally do well in marital therapy and those who can't tolerate a sometimes brutal self-appraisal, do not.

Marriage is the most complicated relationship any of us will ever enter into. As I say in the book, it offers the possibility for both ecstasy and agony. Within its parameters we can have a hedge against loneliness, a partner and friend, companion, playmate, confidant and lover. A good marriage can promote health, happiness and personal growth. A bad marriage can hurt you in every area of your life. It's like having a bad back . . . you can't move without it hurting. I am so hopeful that what you read here will help each of you have the kind of marriage you want. You're in charge. Take the challenge. You can do it.

"Marriage is a lottery."
—*Samuel Smiles*

Bibliography

Ables, Billie S. and Brandsma, Jeffrey M., *Therapy for Couples*, Jossey-Bass Publishers, San Francisco, 1977.

Bader, Ellyn, Ph.D. and Pearson, Peter T., Ph.D., *In Quest of the Mythical Mate*, Brunner/Mazel, New York, 1988.

Beavers, W. Robert, M.D., *Successful Marriage*, W.W. Norton & Company, New York, 1985.

Bettelheim, Bruno and Rosenfeld, Alvin, *The Art of the Obvious*, Alfred A. Knopf, New York, 1986.

Dym, Barry, Ph.D. and Glenn, Michael L., M.D., *Couples: Exploring and Understanding the Cycles of Intimate Relationships*, Harper-Collins, New York, 1993.

Finchem, Frank D., and Bradbury, Thomas N., Editors, *The Psychology of Marriage: Basic Issues and Applications*, The Guilford Press, New York and London, 1990.

Gilbert, Roberta M., M.D., *Extraordinary Relationships: A New Way of Thinking About Human Interactions*, Chronimed Publishing, Minneapolis, 1992.

Haley, Jay, *Problem Solving Therapy*, Jossey-Bass, San Francisco, 1977.

Hendrix, Harville, Ph.D., *Getting the Love You Want,*

Henry Holt And Company, New York, 1988.

Jacobson, Neil S. and Margolin, Gayla, *Marital Therapy: Strategies Based on Social Learning and Behavior Exchange Principles*, Brunner/Mazel, New York, 1979.

Lazarus, Arnold A., Ph.D., *Marital Myths*. Impact Publishers, San Luis Obispo, CA., 1985.

Lederer, William J. and Jackson, Don D., *The Mirages of Marriage*, W.W. Norton & Company, New York, 1985.

Mahler, M.S., *The Psychological Birth of the Human Infant*, Basic Books, New York, 1975.

Markman, Howard; Stanley, Scott; Blumbert, Susan L., *Fighting For Your Marriage*, Jossey-Bass Publishers, San Francisco, 1994.

Rogers, Carl R., Ph.D., *Becoming Partners*, A Delta Book, LaJolla, CA, 1972.

Satir, Virginia, *Conjoint Family Therapy*, Science and Behavior Books, Palo Alto, CA, 1964.

Schnarch, David, Ph.D., *Constructing the Sexual Crucible*, W.W. Norton & Company, New York and London, 1991.

Schnarch, David, Ph.D., *Passionate Marriage*, W.W. Norton & Company, New York and London, 1997.

Schwartz, Lita Linzer and Kaslow, Florence W., *Painful Partings*, John Wiley & Sons, Inc., New York, 1997.

Segreves, R. Taylor, *Marital Therapy: A Combined Psychodynamic — Behavioral Approach*, Plenum Medical Book Co., New York and London, 1982.

Sherman, Robert and Fredman, Norman, *Handbook of Structured Techniques in Marriage and Family Therapy*, Brunner/Mazel Publishers, New York, 1986.

Sholevar, G. Pirooz, M.D., Editor, *The Handbook of Marriage and Marital Therapy*, SP Medical and Scientific Books, New York, 1981.

Solomon, Marion F. Ph.D., *Lean On Me: The Power of Positive Dependency in Intimate Relationships*, Simon & Schuster, New York, 1994.

Weeks, Gerald R., Ph.D. and Treat, Stephen, D. Min., *Couples in Treatment*, Brunner/Mazel Publishers, New York, 1992.

Willi, Jurg, M.D., *Couples in Collusion*, Jason Aronson, New York, 1982.

About the Author

Rebecca F. Ward, MS, MSW, has a private practice in general psychotherapy with a special interest in couples and marital therapy in Little Rock, Arkansas. She is a Board Certified Diplomate in Clinical Social Work and is licensed by both the Social Work Licensing Board and the Arkansas Board of Examiners in Psychology. Her professional associations include clinical memberships in The American Association for Marriage and Family Therapy. American Group Psychotherapy Association and National Association of Social Workers. She belongs to the state associations of each of the above and has served on the boards of all. Appointed by Governors Jim Guy Tucker and Mike Huckabee, she has served on the Social Work Licensing Board since 1996. Currently she is the chairman of the Community Advisory Committee at the University of Arkansas Department of Social Work.

Rebecca has written for several Arkansas newspapers since 1966 and has been published in the Arkansas Times, the Arkansas Democrat-Gazette, and the Arkansas Women's Journal. She teaches a graduate course in theories of marital and family therapy for UALR.

She lives in Little Rock with her husband, Don. They have just finished building a house and swear that the information in *How To Stay Married Without Going Crazy* kept them married and sane. She is addicted to chocolate in any form, the New York Times Crossword Puzzle, and appreciates elastic. ("God gave us elastic to make up for menopause.") She plans a sequel to this first book that will include chapters on infidelity, step-families, and intimacy issues.